College Football Stadiums

To the memory of my twin brother,
Ben Stewart, Jr. (1931–1984) —
Christian, avid college football fan and
reporter for several Southern newspapers

and

to his son Matt Stewart —
college student and aspiring journalist.

College Football Stadiums

An Illustrated Guide to NCAA Division I-A

by
Alva W. Stewart

McFarland & Company, Inc., Publishers
Jefferson, North Carolina, and London

On the cover: Clifford B. and Audry Jones Stadium at Texas Tech University in Lubbock, Texas.

Library of Congress Cataloguing-in-Publication Data

Stewart, Alva W., 1931–
    College football stadiums : an illustrated guide to NCAA division I-A / by Alva W. Stewart.
        p.   cm.
    Includes index.
    ISBN 0-7864-0902-9 (softcover : 50# alkaline paper) ∞
    1. Football stadiums — United States — Directories. 2. Universities and colleges — United States — Directories. I. Title.
GV415.S76   2000
796.332'06'873 — dc21   00-35487
                                                                               CIP

British Library Cataloguing-in-Publication data are available

©2000 Alva W. Stewart. All rights reserved

No part of this book may be reproduced or transmitted in any form or by any means, electronic or mechanical, including photocopying or recording, or by any information storage and retrieval system, without permission in writing from the publisher.

Manufactured in the United States of America

McFarland & Company, Inc., Publishers
  Box 611, Jefferson, North Carolina 28640
    www.mcfarlandpub.com

ACKNOWLEDGMENTS

Scores of individuals, most of whom I have never met, have contributed in large or small measure to this book. Much of the material has come from sports information and media relations directors, their assistants, and interns at the 114 colleges and universities represented in these pages. Some of these have gone above and beyond the call of duty in supplying information and or illustrations. To all of these I am most grateful.

To librarians I owe a special debt of gratitude for their willingness to provide the names and tenure of head football coaches and athletic directors, primarily the latter, at their institutions when this information was unavailable elsewhere. Those in this group are: Lawrence R. Stark, assistant archivist, Washington State University; Maria Davis, University Archives, Bruce T. Halle Library, Eastern Michigan University; Sheppard Black, Special Collections librarian, Ohio University; Jeff Thomas, archivist, Ohio State University Library; Ralph L. Elder, assistant director, Center for American History, University of Texas at Austin; and Donald DeWitt, curator, Western History Collection, University of Oklahoma Library.

Laura Hayworth, library technical assistant, and Mary Katherine Amos, library assistant, Jackson Library, UNC–Greensboro, were both immensely helpful in supplying needed addresses and telephone numbers expeditiously and cheerfully. For providing helpful information on NCAA stadium requirements for Division I-A members I wish to thank Carol Anne Gilmore, assistant director of compliance and championships, Atlantic Coast Conference.

In a project of this magnitude, emotional support from friends and family members is virtually essential to bring it to fruition. I would be remiss not to mention the encouragement given me by Ned Harrison, who, unlike this writer, never had any doubt that the book would be published. Another person who reassured me of the project's value and offered timely advice on several occasions was Herb Appenzeller, author and athletics director emeritus at Guilford College in Greensboro. Several other friends extended their support by inquiring as to the progress of the work during its gestation period. To computer guru and friend John Newton I am grateful for technical aid to a computer neophyte.

Last but certainly not least I must express my sincere gratitude to my wife Margaret for her unfailing encouragement along a sometimes rocky path and for understanding my long-standing wish to write something more enduring than an article for a travel magazine. In a book of this nature it is inevitable that some factual inaccuracies will occur. I have made every effort to minimize these errors and willingly accept responsibility for any which appear in the following pages.

ILLUSTRATION CREDITS

Illustrations (photographs, logos, slides, and CDs) which appear in this book were kindly provided by the following sources:

Sports information offices from the following universities: Akron, Alabama–Tuscaloosa, Alabama–Birmingham, Arkansas State, Ball State, Bowling Green State, Boise State, Boston College, Brigham Young, Central Florida, Central Michigan, Cincinnati, Colorado, Duke, East Carolina, Eastern Michigan, Florida, Florida State, Fresno State, Georgia Tech, Kansas, Kansas State, Kent State, Louisiana State, Louisville, Marshall, Maryland, Miami, Michigan State, Mississippi, Missouri, Nevada–Reno, North Carolina State, North Texas, Northeast Louisiana, Northern Illinois, Notre Dame, Ohio, Oregon State, Purdue, Rice, South Carolina, Southern California, Southern Mississippi, Southwestern Louisiana, Texas A&M, Texas–Austin, Texas Christian, Texas–El Paso, Toledo, Tulsa, U.S. Military Academy, U.S. Naval Academy, Utah, Virginia Polytechnic Institute, Wake Forest, Western Michigan, Wisconsin, and Wyoming.

Media relations and athletic media relations offices from the following universities: Arizona, Arizona State, Arkansas, Auburn, Baylor, California–Berkeley, California–Los Angeles, Hawaii, Idaho, Illinois, Indiana, Iowa State, Louisiana Tech, Memphis, Middle Tennessee State, Minnesota, Mississippi State, New Mexico, New Mexico State, Northwestern, Oklahoma, Oklahoma State, Oregon, Pittsburgh, Rutgers, San Diego State, San Jose State, Stanford, Temple, Tulane, Utah State, Vanderbilt, Washington, and Washington State.

Director of Athletics and Athletic Departments from the following universities: Clemson, Colorado State, Houston, and Miami (Ohio).

Photographers: Kent Gidley, Univ. of Alabama; Scott Photography, Scottsdale, Arizona; Patrick Merrill, Univ. of California–Berkeley; Jim Graham, Anderson, South Carolina; David Coyle, Univ. of Kentucky; University Photographer, Univ. of North Carolina; University Photographer, North Carolina State Univ.; Photography Center, Univ. of Tennessee; Photo Services, Univ. of Michigan; Daniel Grogan, Charlottesville, Virginia; and Pete Emerson, Waynesboro, Virginia.

Other Sources: Athletic Communications, SUNY–Buffalo; Audio-Visual Center, SUNY–Buffalo; Pasadena Tournament of Roses; Sports Communications, Univ. of Georgia; Athletics Association, Univ. of Kentucky; Athletics Association, U.S. Air Force Academy; News & Information Services, Univ. of Michigan; Athletic Licensing & Sales, Univ. of Nebraska; Promotions Office, Univ. of Nevada–Las Vegas; Dept. of Auxiliary Services, Univ. of North Carolina; Licensing Office, Ohio State Univ.; Photo/Graphics, Pennsylvania State Univ.; Athletic Marketing Dept., Southern Methodist University; Athletic Communications, Syracuse Univ.; University Relations, Univ. of Virginia; and News and Information Services, West Virginia University.

CONTENTS

Acknowledgments v
Illustration Credits vi
Preface 1

THE STADIUMS

University of Akron	6
University of Alabama	8
University of Alabama–Birmingham	10
University of Arizona	12
Arizona State University	14
University of Arkansas	16
Arkansas State University	18
Auburn University	20
Ball State University	22
Baylor University	24
Boise State University	26
Boston College	28
Bowling Green State University	30
Brigham Young University	32
State University of New York at Buffalo	34
University of California–Berkeley	36
University of California–Los Angeles	38
University of Central Florida	40
Central Michigan University	42
University of Cincinnati	44
Clemson University	46
University of Colorado	48
Colorado State University	50
Duke University	52
East Carolina University	54
Eastern Michigan University	56

University of Florida	58
Florida State University	60
Fresno State University	62
University of Georgia	64
Georgia Institute of Technology	66
University of Hawaii	68
University of Houston	70
University of Idaho	72
University of Illinois	74
Indiana University	76
University of Iowa	78
Iowa State University	80
University of Kansas	82
Kansas State University	84
Kent State University	86
University of Kentucky	88
Louisiana State University	90
Louisiana Tech University	92
University of Louisville	94
Marshall University	96
University of Maryland	98
University of Memphis	100
University of Miami	102
Miami University	104
University of Michigan	106
Michigan State University	108
Middle Tennessee State University	110
University of Minnesota	112
University of Mississippi	114
Mississippi State University	116
University of Missouri	118
University of Nebraska	120
University of Nevada–Las Vegas	122
University of Nevada–Reno	124
University of New Mexico	126
New Mexico State University	128
University of North Carolina	130
North Carolina State University	132
University of North Texas	134
Northeast Louisiana University	136

Northern Illinois University	138
Northwestern University	140
University of Notre Dame	142
Ohio State University	144
Ohio University	146
University of Oklahoma	148
Oklahoma State University	150
University of Oregon	152
Oregon State University	154
Pennsylvania State University	156
University of Pittsburgh	158
Purdue University	160
Rice University	162
Rutgers University	164
San Diego State University	166
San Jose State University	168
University of South Carolina	170
University of Southern California	172
Southern Methodist University	174
University of Southern Mississippi	176
University of Southwestern Louisiana	178
Stanford University	180
Syracuse University	182
Temple University	184
University of Tennessee	186
University of Texas–Austin	188
University of Texas–El Paso	190
Texas A&M University	192
Texas Christian University	194
Texas Tech University	196
University of Toledo	198
Tulane University	200
University of Tulsa	202
United States Air Force Academy	204
United States Military Academy	206
United States Naval Academy	208
University of Utah	210
Utah State University	212
Vanderbilt University	214
University of Virginia	216

Virginia Polytechnic Institute & State University	218
Wake Forest University	220
University of Washington	222
Washington State University	224
West Virginia University	226
Western Michigan University	228
University of Wisconsin	230
University of Wyoming	232
Index	235

PREFACE

For more than a century, college football has been one of the most colorful, spirited, and exciting sports in the world. The game itself, demanding skills, strength, and endurance, evokes the essentials of drama: suspense, competition, triumph, and failure. It is a game which has stirred an American president to save it — Theodore Roosevelt; another to coach it — Woodrow Wilson; and a third to play and coach it — Dwight Eisenhower. Other presidents who played college football were Richard M. Nixon, Gerald Ford, and Ronald Reagan.

College football games are played in stadiums (or, stadia) — some large, some small; some with luxury suites, others without such amenities. In the following pages I have attempted to provide basic information on stadiums used by the 114 colleges and universities who are members of NCAA Division I-A.

This information was supplied by staff members in the sports information and media relations offices of the schools represented. To obtain it, a questionnaire was mailed to the sports information director of each school in January 1999. If the questionnaire was not returned in two months, a follow-up questionnaire was mailed. Those 20+ SIDs who did not respond to either the original or follow-up questionnaire were called and requested to complete the questionnaire and return it to me. By November 1, 1999, each of the 114 schools had responded in some fashion. In addition to information about the stadium, each was asked to send photos or slides of the stadium, team mascot or logo, and a well-known campus landmark to illustrate the factual data. With few exceptions the sports information directors or other athletic office staff member provided the needed information and illustrations. In several instances I extracted the data from media guides sent to me.

An even dozen athletic conferences are represented by the 114 teams. They are: Big Ten, Atlantic Coast, Southeastern, Big 12, Pacific-10, Big East, Mid-American, Western Athletic, Mountain West, Big West, Conference USA, and Sun Belt. Less than half a dozen of the schools are independents.

Many schools have a name for their playing field which is different from that of the stadium. Because of possible confusion, I decided against inclusion of field names. Almost half of the stadiums are named for an individual, in many cases a former coach or benefactor of the college. Several are named in memory of war veterans. In those few instances where the stadium name has changed since its opening, both the original and current name have been given. The oldest stadium is Bobby Dodd Stadium at Georgia Tech, which opened in 1913. The newest is Southern Methodist University, where stadium seats will be occupied for the first time in the Fall of 2000. The overwhelming majority of stadiums opened prior to 1975.

A few of the schools are members of one conference as far as football is concerned but belong to another conference with regard to other sports. In these pages only the football conference affiliation is noted. More than half of the teams played their first football game in the last two decades of the 19th century. The first game was played in 1869, when Rutgers defeated Princeton 6–4. Every team played its first game prior to 1960.

Seating capacity varies from 17,000 to more than 100,000, with the average capacity of the 114 stadiums approximately 55,000. The NCAA requires Division I-A members to play in a stadium with a minimum of 30,000 permanent seats *or* to "have averaged more than 17,000 in paid attendance per home football game in the immediate past four-year period." About nine-tenths of the schools' stadiums are on campus. Of those teams who play their home games off campus, the distance between campus and stadium is only a few miles or less. Several of these off-campus stadiums are owned and operated by an entity other than the college or university. Examples of these are UCLA, whose team plays in the Rose Bowl, and the University of Miami, whose home stadium is the Orange Bowl.

Except for a dozen or so, all stadiums have lights. In almost all cases where no lighting system is available, the stadium is relatively small and no games are televised there. The number of teams whose fields have natural grass only slightly exceeds those who have artificial turf. Most of the schools have experimented with both types of playing surfaces over the years.

The majority of stadiums are used for both football games and other events such as commencement exercises, track meets, and concerts. Several have been the sites of Super Bowl games and Summer Olympic Games competition. Others have been the venue for annual postseason college games such as the Orange Bowl.

Readers who compare the cost of stadium construction, additions, and renovations will observe the wide discrepancy of cost prior to 1950 and the post–1950 years. Unfortunately, many of the schools did not report cost figures, either because they were not readily available or they chose not to release these figures for public consumption. The same reason applies to the lack of data on the method of financing these costs.

Special features of stadiums cover a wide spectrum ranging from a multi-level press box to the burial site of several University of Georgia bulldogs who served as the team mascot. Team mascots are as diverse as team names. Frequently the two are linked; e.g., the Arkansas Razorbacks (name) have a wild hog, or razorback, as their mascot. In a few instances, such as Miami (Ohio) University, the mascot has a distinctive name ("Swoop"). In most cases the mascot is a costumed figure; however, in several, it is a live animal such as the ram at the University of North Carolina.

Colors vary widely, with the most common being blue and white or red and white. Some schools specify a particular shade of a color; others do not. The most unusual colors are probably cream, cardinal red, and emerald green.

It is my hope that listing all head coaches and athletic directors, with tenure for each, since the stadium opened will have historical value to readers. In two or three instances, this information was not supplied, presumably because it was not readily available. Individual tenure of both coaches and athletic directors varies from one year to more than 25 years, with a few individuals serving simultaneously in both positions. As any college football fan might expect, 100 percent of the coaches, past and present, are males. However, the same is not true of the athletic directors, where a close scrutiny of names reveals a few females — fewer than 2 percent. The latter development is a recent one but one that is likely to continue, with even larger numbers of females in the 21st century. Joe Paterno of Penn State holds the record for the longest tenure as head coach of any Division I-A team — since 1966. Interim coaches are not included in these lists since almost all of them had tenure of less than a year. Individuals identified as the current coach or athletic director held that position as of January 15, 2000.

Some sports information directors insisted on a letter from the publisher before lending photos for use in the book, while others required payment in advance. In some instances I was referred to another office on campus, or in several cases, to an office off campus where the stadium was located. Fortunately, in only one or two cases were no illustrations available for a school.

Because of a self-imposed deadline the cutoff date for inclusion of schools in the book was December 1, 1999. Any schools admitted to NCAA Division I-A membership since that date are excluded for this reason only.

My aim throughout this project has been to treat each of the 114 schools equitably. I hope I have attained that goal.

Al Stewart
Greensboro, North Carolina
February 2000

THE STADIUMS

UNIVERSITY OF AKRON
Akron, Ohio

Rubber Bowl (1940)

Lights: Yes. *Seating capacity:* 35,202. *Location:* Off campus. *Playing surface:* Artificial turf. *Special features:* Locker rooms, press box. Stadium is the largest in the Mid-American Conference. *Other uses:* Regular season as well as state high school championship games are played here. Occasional concerts are held here.

Original construction: 1939, cost not reported but financed by a federal grant and private donations. *Additions and renovations:* In 1971 the lighting system was improved. Astroturf was installed in 1973 and a new scoreboard was erected in 1991. Improvements in 1994 included installation of a new drainage system, a complete paint job, and refurbished stands. Cost of these renovations totaled $1.9 million. They were financed by a fund-raising drive, a bond issue, and University funds.

Team name: Zips. *Team mascot:* Zippy the Kangaroo (costumed figure). *Colors:* Blue and gold. *Song:* "Akron Blue and Gold." *Conference:* Mid-American. *First intercollegiate football game:* 1940.

Coaches and their tenure: Thomas Dowler (1940), Otis W. Douglas (1941–42), No games played during period 1943–45, Paul Baldacci (1946–47), William "Bud" Houghton (1948–51), Kenneth "Red" Cochrane (1952–53), Joseph H. McMullen (1954–60), Gordon K. Larson (1961–72), James Dennison (1973–85), Gerry Faust (1986–94), Lee Owens (1995–).

Athletic directors and their tenure: Leslie P. Hardy (1940–42), Otis Douglas (1943), Leslie Hardy (1944–45), Russ Beichly (1946–47), Kenneth "Red" Cochrane (1948–69), Gordon K. Larson (1970–84), Dave Adams (1985–87), Jim Dennison (1988–94), Michael Bobinski (1995–98), Dennis Helsel (1999–).

Zippy the Kangaroo

UNIVERSITY OF ALABAMA
Tuscaloosa, Alabama

Bryant-Denny Stadium (1929)

Named for Paul "Bear" Bryant, head football coach for more than 25 years at the University, and Dr. George Denny, former president of the University. **Lights:** Yes. **Seating capacity:** 83,818. **Location:** On campus. **Playing surface:** Grass. **Special features:** Locker rooms, press box, luxury suites, and scoreboard with video replay capability. **Other uses:** Luxury suites are used for luncheons and meetings at various times throughout the year.
Original construction: 1929, cost not reported. **Additions and renovations:** Additional seats were erected in 1937, 1950, 1961, 1966, and 1988. In 1961 a press box was constructed. The largest expansion came in 1998 with the addition of 13,500 seats, 81 sky boxes on two levels, and two reception areas for Scholarship and A-Club patrons. A new scoreboard was also installed in 1998. Cost of these improvements was not reported, nor was the method of financing this cost.
Team name: Crimson Tide. **Team mascot:** Big Al (costumed figure dressed as elephant). **Colors:** Crimson and white. **Song:** "Yea Alabama." **Conference:** Southeastern. **First intercollegiate football game:** 1892.
Coaches and their tenure: Wallace Wade (1929–30), Frank Thomas (1931–46), Harold "Red" Drew (1947–54), J.B. Whitworth (1955–57), Paul "Bear" Bryant (1958–82), Ray Perkins (1983–86), Bill Curry (1987–89), Gene Stallings (1990–96), Mike DuBose (1997–).
Athletic directors and their tenure: Wallace Wade (1929–30), Frank Thomas (1931–52), Pete Cawthon (1953), Hank Crisp (1954–57), Paul W. Bryant (1958–82), Ray Perkins (1983–86), Steve Sloan (1987–88), Hootie Ingram (1989–95), Bob Bockrath (1996–1999), Mel Moore (2000–).

Big Al

UNIVERSITY OF ALABAMA–BIRMINGHAM
Birmingham, Alabama

Legion Field (1927)
Named in honor of the American Legion and stands as a memorial to Americans killed in service to their country. The Birmingham Park Board is responsible for stadium operation and maintenance.
Lights: Yes. *Seating capacity:* 80,391. *Location:* Off campus. *Playing surface:* Grass. *Special features:* Locker rooms, weight and conditioning rooms, coaches' offices, and luxury suites. *Other uses:* Site of first round of soccer games in the 1996 Summer Olympic Games. Stadium has been the home field for four professional football teams during the past 25 years.
Original construction: 1926, at a cost of $439,000. *Additions and renovations:* Over the years the seating capacity has been expanded to four times its original size. The last addition and renovation occurred in 1990, when a new press box was built and two luxury suites and 12 skyboxes were added to increase total seating in all suites and skyboxes to 900. Financing of these improvements was made possible by the city's issuance of bonds.
Team name: Blazers. *Team mascot:* Blaze. *Colors:* Forest green and old gold. *Song:* None. *Conference:* Conference USA. *First intercollegiate football game:* 1991.
Coaches and their tenure: Dr. Jim Hilyer (1991–94), Watson Brown (1995–).
Athletic directors and their tenure: Gene Bartow (1991–).

Logo for University of Alabama–Birmingham Blazers

UNIVERSITY OF ARIZONA
Tucson, Arizona

Arizona Stadium (1929)

Lights: Yes. **Seating capacity**: 57,803. **Location:** On campus. **Playing surface**: Natural grass (Bermuda tiff). **Special features**: Scoreboard featuring full-color animation and display capabilities, four-story skybox with media center seating 103 working press members on 4th level. Every seat in stadium has an uncluttered view of playing surface and more than half the seats have a sweeping view of the Santa Catalina Mountains. **Other uses**: Home to annual Insight.com Bowl each December; host to Arizona high school playoffs each year. **Original construction**: 1928, cost not reported. **Additions and renovations**: In 1938, 3,000 seats were added on east side, with horseshoe completed at south end in 1950. Construction of press box and addition of 10,000 seats took place in 1965. Two-tier addition to east stands occurred in 1976 and permanent bleacher seating for 4,500 was added in 1989. In 1998 "Ring of Fame" was installed to honor outstanding former players along the façade of east side upper deck. Cost of 1989 addition was $6.3 million. **Projected addition:** None planned.
Team name: Wildcats. **Team mascot**: Wilma the Wildcat. **Colors**: Cardinal red and navy blue. **Song**: "Bear Down, Arizona." **Conference**: Pacific-10. **First intercollegiate football game:** 1899.
Coaches and their tenure: J.F. "Pop" Mc-Kale (1929–30), Fred A. Enke (1931), A.W. "Gus" Farwick (1932), G.A. "Tex" Oliver (1933–37), Orlan M Landreth (1938), Miles W. Casteel (1939–42, 1945–48), Robert E. Winslow (1949–51), Warren Woodson (1952–56), Edward A. Doherty (1957–58), Jim LaRue (1959–66), Darrell Mudra (1967–68), Robert W. Weber (1969–72), James C. Young (1973–76), Tony Mason (1977–79), Larry Smith (1980–86), Dick Tomey (1987–).
Athletic directors and their tenure: James F. "Pop" McKale (1929–57), M.R. (Dick) Clausen (1958–72), David Strack (1973–81), Cedric Dempsey (1982–94), Jim Livengood (1995–).

Wilma the Wildcat

Arizona State University
Tempe, Arizona

Sun Devil Stadium (1958)

Lights: Yes. *Seating capacity:* 73,379. *Location:* On campus. *Special features:* Press box, eight private suites, scoreboard with state-of-the-art video replay system, four elevators, 383 seats for physically disabled spectators, and TV production room. *Playing surface*: Natural grass. *Other uses*: Super Bowl was played here in the late 1980s. Stadium has been home to Fiesta Bowl for 20 years. Arizona Cardinals (NFL) play their home games here.
Original construction: 1958, cost not reported. *Additions and renovations*: In 1976, 1977, and 1988 seating capacity was expanded. The Intercollegiate Athletic Complex housing the entire ASU Athletic Department was added to the stadium's south end in 1988 at a cost of $11 million. *Projected additions*: Plans have been developed to enlarge seating capacity to a figure between 80 and 90,000. Estimated cost of this addition is more than $20 million. Addition in 1988 was financed by revenue bonds, private donations, ticket surcharge, and a grant from the Sun Angel Foundation, a support group for ASU athletic programs.
Team name: Sun Devils. *Team mascot*: Sun Devil. *Colors*: Maroon and gold. *Song*: None. *Conference*: Pacific-10. *First intercollegiate football game:* 1897.
Coaches and their tenure: Frank Kush (1958–79), Darryl Rogers (1980), John Cooper (1985–87), Larry Marmie (1988–91), Bruce Snyder (1992–).
Athletic directors and their tenure: Clyde B. Smith (1958–70), Fred L. Miller (1971–80), Dick Tamburo (1981–83), Frank Sarklon (1984–85), Charles Harris (1986–95), Dr. Kevin White (1996–).

Logo for ASU's Sun Devil

UNIVERSITY OF ARKANSAS
Fayetteville, Arkansas

Razorback Stadium (1938)

Lights: Yes. *Seating capacity:* 50,000. *Location:* On campus. *Special features:* Press box, luxury seats. *Playing surface:* Natural grass. *Other uses:* None. *Original construction:* 1938, cost not reported. *Additions and renovations:* Between 2,500 and 5,200 seats were added in each of the following years: 1947, 1950, 1957, and 1965. In 1969 seating capacity was increased to 42,678. In 1975 the Broyles Athletic Center was built with offices for coaches and athletic administrators. An extensive renovation of the Center occurred in 1994. Cost of these additions and renovation was not reported; neither was the method of financing this cost.
Team name: Razorbacks. *Team mascot:* Razorback (wild hog). *Colors:* Cardinal and white. *Song:* "Arkansas Fight Song." *Conference:* Southeastern. *First intercollegiate football game:* 1894.
Coaches and their tenure: Fred Thomsen (1938–41), George Cole (1942), John Tomlin (1943), Glen Rose (1944–45), John Barnhill (1946–49), Otis Douglas (1950–52), Bowden Wyatt (1953–54), Jack Mitchell (1955–57), Frank Broyles (1958–76), Lou Holtz (1977–83), Ken Hatfield (1984–89), Jack Crowe (1990–91), Joe Kines (1992), Danny Ford (1993–97), Houston Nutt (1998–).
Athletic directors and their tenure: The first athletic director was appointed in 1946. John Barnhill (1946–70), George Cole (1971–72), Frank Broyles (1973–99), Rick Shaeffer (2000–).

University of Arkansas' Razorback

1993 Indian Football Schedule

Date	Opponent	Time
Sept. 5	at Minnesota	1:30 p.m.
Sept. 12	at Louisiana State	7 p.m.
Sept. 19	SOUTHWEST MISSOURI STATE	1 p.m.
Sept. 26	at Hawai'i	11 p.m.
Oct. 3	NEW MEXICO STATE (Homecoming)	1 p.m.
Oct. 10	IDAHO	1 p.m.
Oct. 17	at Southwestern Louisiana	4 p.m.
Oct. 24	at Mississippi	1 p.m.
Oct. 31	at Memphis	1 p.m.
Nov. 7	LOUISIANA TECH	1 p.m.
Nov. 14	NORTHEAST LOUISIANA	1 p.m.
Nov. 21	CINCINNATI	1 p.m.

ARKANSAS STATE UNIVERSITY
State University, Arkansas

Indian Stadium (1974)

Lights: Yes. *Seating capacity:* 33,410. *Location:* On campus. *Playing surface:* Grass. *Special features:* Locker rooms, press box, coaches' offices, and meeting/conference room. *Other uses:* None.
Original construction: 1974, at a cost of $2.5 million. *Additions and renovations:* In 1992 seats were added to meet NCAA Division I-A requirements for membership, bringing capacity to current figure. Cost of this addition was not reported; it was financed through a state appropriation and private donations.
Team name: Indians. *Team mascot:* Indian family of three, including Chief Big Track, a brave, and a princess. *Colors:* Scarlet and black. *Song:* "On, On, On to Victory." *Conference:* Big West. *First intercollegiate football game:* 1911.
Coaches and their tenure: Bill Davidson (1974–78), Larry Lacewell (1979–89), Al Kincaid (1990–91), Ray Perkins (1992), John Bobo (1993–96), Joe Hollis (1997–).
Athletic directors and their tenure: Don Floyd (1974–75), Dean Pryor (1976–79), Larry Lacewell (1980–90), Charley Thornton (1991–93), Dr. Brad Hovious (1994–95), Barry Dowd (1996–).

Indian family of three consisting of a brave, Chief Big Track, and a princess

AUBURN UNIVERSITY
Auburn, Alabama

Jordan-Hare Stadium (1939)

Named after Cliff Hare, a member of Auburn's first football team, president of the old Southern Conference, and longtime chairman of Auburn's Faculty Athletic Committee, and Ralph "Shug" Jordan, the University's all-time winningest football coach.
Lights: Yes. **Seating capacity:** 85,214. **Location:** On campus. **Playing surface:** Natural grass. **Special features:** 68 luxury suites located under east upper deck, locker rooms, and press box. **Other uses:** None.
Original construction: 1939, cost not reported; method of financing cost not reported. **Additions and renovations:** West side upper deck was added in 1980 and east side upper deck was completed in 1987. In 1998 a new scoreboard featuring live telecast and instant replay capabilities was installed. Cost of these improvements was $30 million. Source of financing this cost was not reported.
Team name: Tigers. **Team mascot:** (1) "Aubie," a costumed tiger, and (2) "Tiger," a golden eagle. **Colors:** Burnt orange and navy blue. **Song:** "War Eagle." **Conference:** Southeastern. **First intercollegiate football game:** 1892.
Coaches and their tenure: Jack Meagher (1939–43), Carl Voyles (1944–47), Earl Brown (1948–50), Ralph Jordan (1951–75), Doug Barfield (1976–80), Pat Dye (1981–92), Terry Bowden (1993–98), Tommy Tuberville (1999–).
Athletic directors and their tenure: Jack Meagher (1939–43), Carl Voyles (1944–47), Wilbur Hutsell (1948–50), Jeff Beard (1951–72), Lee Haley (1973–81), Pat Dye (1982–92), Mike Lude (1993–94), David Housel (1995–).

Auburn's costumed mascot — Aubie

BALL STATE UNIVERSITY
Muncie, Indiana

Ball State University Stadium (1967)

Lights: No. *Seating capacity:* 21,581. *Location:* On campus. *Special features:* Press box. *Playing surface:* Grass. *Other uses:* None.

Original construction: 1967, cost not reported. *Additions and renovations:* Upgraded seating capacity on east side of stadium in 1995 at estimated cost of $10–15 million. *Projected additions:* Construction of new press box, completion of new football building in end zone, and expansion of seating capacity to 30,000 are improvements being made in 2000. Cost of these improvements was not reported. Private gifts financed 1995 addition as well as renovation in 2000.

Team name: Cardinals. *Team mascot:* Cardinal (Charlie). *Colors:* Cardinal and white. *Song:* "Ball State Fight Song." *Conference:* Mid-American. *First intercollegiate football game:* 1924. *Coaches and their tenure:* Ray Louthern (1967), Wave Myers (1968–70), Dave McClain (1971–77), Dwight Wallace (1978–84), Paul Schudel (1985–94), Bill Lynch (1995–). *Athletic directors and their tenure:* Bob Primmer (1967–70), Ray Louthen (1971–81), Dwight Wallace (1982–84), Don Purvis (1985–95), Andrea Seger (1996–).

Charlie Cardinal

BAYLOR UNIVERSITY
Waco, Texas

Floyd Casey Stadium (1950)

Formerly Baylor Stadium, it was renamed Floyd Casey Stadium in 1989 to honor the father of long-time University trustee and supporter Carl B. Casey. He and his wife Thelma contributed $5 million toward stadium renovation.
Lights: Yes. *Seating capacity:* 50,000. *Location:* Off campus. *Playing surface:* Grass. *Special features:* Locker rooms, press box, luxury suites, and coaches' offices. *Other uses:* None.
Original construction: 1950, cost not reported. *Additions and renovations:* Astroturf installed in 1972, again in 1979, with all-pro turf laid in 1989. In June 1998 Baylor removed the artificial turf and replaced it with Sport Grass. Lights replaced in 1996. In 1999 press box was enlarged on west side of stadium. Bear Foundation seating level for scholarship donors was expanded. Number of luxury suites was increased to 37, each containing 8–16 seats, refrigerator, television set, and offering catered meals. Cost of these improvements was $9 million. Private donations paid for all improvements.
Team name: Bears. *Team mascot:* Bear (costumed figure). *Colors:* Green and gold. *Song:* "Old Fight." *Conference:* Big 12. *First intercollegiate football game:* 1899.
Coaches and their tenure: George Sauer (1950–55), Sam Boyd (1956–58), John Bridgers (1959–68), Bill Beall (1969–71), Grant Teaff (1972–92), Chuck Reedy (1993–95), Dave Roberts (1996–97), Kevin Steele (1998–).
Athletic directors and their tenure: George Sauer (1950–58), John Bridgers (1959–67), Bill Henderson (1968–71), Jack Patterson (1972–81), Bill Menefee (1981–92), Dick Ellis (1993–96), Tom Stanton (1997–).

Logo for Baylor University Bears

BOISE STATE UNIVERSITY
Boise, Idaho

Bronco Stadium (1970)

Lights: Yes. ***Seating capacity:*** 30,000. ***Location:*** On campus. ***Playing surface:*** Blue Astroturf. ***Special features:*** None. ***Other uses:*** Track and field meets. ***Original construction:*** 1970 at a cost of $2,252,750. ***Additions and renovations:*** East side upper deck was added in 1974 and south end zone addition was completed in 1997. Addition in 1974 cost $1,579,200, and 1997 addition cost $9,350,000. Financing of both additions was done through private donations and Athletic Department funds. No projected addition is planned.
Team name: Broncos. ***Team mascot:*** Bronco. ***Colors:*** Blue and orange. ***Song:*** "BSU Fight Song." ***Conference:*** Big West. ***First intercollegiate football game:*** 1932.
Coaches and their tenure: Tony Knap (1970–75), Jim Criner (1976–82), Lyle Setencich (l983–86), Skip Hall (1987–92), Pokey Allen (1993–96), Houston Nutt (1997), Dirk Koetter (1998–).
Athletic directors and their tenure: Lyle Smith (1970–80), Mike Mullally (1981), Gene Bleymaier (1982–).

BOSTON COLLEGE
Chestnut Hill, Massachusetts

Alumni Stadium (1957)
Named for all Boston College alumni.
Lights: Yes. **Seating capacity:** 44,500. **Location:** On campus. **Playing surface:** Astroturf 1200. **Special features:** Two-level press box with seating for 100 news media representatives, west side upper deck with 13 luxury boxes, east side with 17 luxury boxes, offers view of Boston skyline. **Other uses:** None.
Original construction: 1957, at a cost of $250,000. **Additions and renovations:** Expansion of seating capacity to 32,000 in 1971. In 1994 12,000 seats were added, new color scoreboards and instant replay screens were erected, new and improved lighting system was installed, and state-of-the-art public address system was installed. Cost of these improvements was not reported, with private donations the method of financing them.
Team name: Eagles. **Team mascot:** Eagle (costumed figure). **Colors:** Maroon and gold. **Song:** "For Boston." **Conference:** Big East. **First intercollegiate football game:** 1898.
Coaches and their tenure: Mike Holovak (1957–59), Ernie Heffer (1960–61), Jim Miller (1962–67), Joe Yukika (1968–77), Ed Chlebek (1978–80), Jack Bicknell (1981–90), Tom Coughlin (1991–93), Dan Henning (1994–96), Tom O'Brien (1997–).
Athletic directors and their tenure: William J. Flynn (1957–91), Gene DeFilippo (1992–).

Boston College's mascot Eagle

BOWLING GREEN STATE UNIVERSITY
Bowling Green, Ohio

Doyt L. Perry Stadium (1966)

Named for former head football coach and athletic director Doyt L. Perry. ***Lights:*** No. ***Seating capacity:*** 30,599. ***Location:*** On campus. ***Playing surface:*** Natural grass. ***Special features:*** Locker rooms, equipment room, weight room/fitness center, maintenance area, luxury suites, and Athletic Department offices. ***Other uses:*** Formerly used for commencement exercises but no longer used for this purpose.
Original construction: 1965, at a cost of $3 million. Method of financing cost not reported. ***Additions and renovations:*** Bleacher-type seats were added in 1982 to increase capacity to current figure. In 1997 elevators were installed on both sides and luxury suites were refurbished. Cost of these improvements was not reported. Their cost was financed with private donations and federal funds authorized by the Americans with Disabilities Act.
Team name: Falcons. ***Mascot:*** Freddie and Frieda Falcon, costumed figures. ***Colors:*** Orange and brown. ***Song:*** "Forward Falcons." ***Conference:*** Mid-American. ***First intercollegiate football game:*** 1919.
Coaches and their tenure: Doyt L. Perry (1955–64), Bob Gibson (1965–67), Don Nehlen (1968–76), Denny Stolz (1977–85), Moe Ankney (1986–90), Gary Blackney (1991–).
Athletic directors and their tenure: Doyt Perry (1965–71), Dr. Robert Bell (1972), Richard Young (1973–78), James Lessig (1979–82), Jack Gregory (1983–94), Ron Zweierlein (1995–).

Freddie and Frieda Falcon

BRIGHAM YOUNG UNIVERSITY
Provo, Utah

Cougar Stadium (1964)

Lights: Yes. **Seating capacity:** 65,000. **Location:** On campus. **Playing surface:** Grass. **Special features:** 42 luxury suites in a spacious press box which seats 95, locker rooms. **Other uses:** Occasional concerts.
Original construction: 1964, cost not reported. **Additions and renovations:** Added 30,000 seats in end zones to bring seating capacity to current figure, lowered playing field, removed track, and built press box in 1982. Cost of these improvements was $15 million. Financing was made possible by private donations and payment of fees for luxury boxes and donor seats.
Team name: Cougars. **Team mascot:** Cosmo the Cougar. **Colors:** Blue and white. **Song:** "Rise and Shout." **Conference:** Mountain West.
First intercollegiate football game: 1922.
Coaches and their tenure: LaVell Edwards (1972–).
Athletic directors and their tenure: Glen Tuckett (1976–93), Clayne Jensen (1994–95), Rondo Fehlberg (1996–).

Cosmo the Cougar

STATE UNIVERSITY OF NEW YORK AT BUFFALO
Buffalo, New York

UB Stadium (1993)

Lights: Yes. **Seating capacity:** 14,000. **Location:** On campus. **Playing surface:** Grass. **Special features:** 45-seat press box with 12 luxury suites. Two large locker rooms can accommodate 800 athletes. Athletic Department offices are housed here, as well as meeting rooms, and state-of-the-art training facilities, including physical conditioning equipment. **Other uses:** Track and field meets.
Original construction: 1993 at a cost of $23 million. **Additions and renovations:** Including seats in both end zones, 14,000 seats were added to bring seating capacity to current figure. Cost of original construction was financed by the New York State Dormitory Authority, with cost of 1999 addition financed by state appropriations and University Athletic Department funds.
Team name: Bulls. **Team mascot:** Victor E. Bull. **Colors:** Royal blue and white. **Song:** Not reported. **Conference:** Mid-American. **First intercollegiate football game:** 1894.
Coaches and their tenure: Jim Ward (1993–94), Craig Cirbus (1995–).
Athletic directors and their tenure: Nelson Townsend (1993–98), Bob Arkeilpane (1999–).

Victor E. Bull

University of California–Berkeley

UNIVERSITY OF CALIFORNIA–BERKELEY
Berkeley, California

Memorial Stadium (1923)

Lights: No. **Seating capacity:** 75,028. **Location:** On campus. **Playing surface:** Grass. **Special features:** Locker rooms, coaches and administrative offices, team meeting and dining room. **Other uses:** Soccer and women's lacrosse games. **Original construction:** 1921, at cost of $1.4 million. **Additions and renovations:** In 1983 training quarters, locker rooms, and weight room were updated and a new administrative complex was constructed. Weight room and training facilities were expanded in 1991. Team meeting room was expanded in 1994. Cost of these improvements was not reported. All improvements were financed through private donations.

Team name: Golden Bears. **Team mascot:** Bear. **Colors:** Blue and gold. **Song:** "Fight for California." **Conference:** Pacific-10. **First intercollegiate football game:** 1882.

Coaches and their tenure: Andy Smith (1923–25), Nibs Price (1926–30), Bill Ingram (1931–34), Stub Allison (1935–44), Buck Shaw (1945), Lynn Waldorf (1947–56), Pete Elliott (1957–59), Marv Levy (1960–63), Ray Willsey (1964–71), Mike White (1972–77), Roger Theder (1978–81), Joe Kapp (1982–86), Bruce Snyder (1987–91), Keith Gilbertson (1992–95), Steve Mariucco (1996), Tom Holmoe (1997–).

Athletic directors and their tenure: Luther A. Nichols (1923–26), W.W. "Bill" Monahan (1927–35), Kenneth Priestly (1936–42), Clint Evans (1943–46), Brutis Hamilton (1947–55), Greg Engelhardt (1956–60), Pete Newell (1961–68), Paul Brechler (1969–72), Dave Maggard (1973–92), Robert Bockrath (1993–94), John Kasser (1995–).

Berkeley's Golden Bear

University of California– Los Angeles
Los Angeles, California

Rose Bowl (1922)

UCLA has used the Rose Bowl as its home stadium since 1982.
Lights: Yes. *Seating capacity:* 92,000. *Location:* Off campus. *Playing surface:* Grass. *Special features:* Locker rooms, luxury suites, coaches' offices, press box, video scoreboards. *Other uses:* Professional soccer team plays its home games here. Flea market is held here once each month.
Original construction: 1922, at a cost of $272,198. Although the Rose Bowl opened in 1922, the Bruins did not begin using it as their home stadium until 1982. *Additions and renovations:* In 1929 the horseshoe shaped stadium was fully closed off. Additional seats were erected in 1932 and again in 1949. Since then multiple renovations have been made to one of the nation's oldest stadiums. Cost of these improvements, which have been financed through seat subscriptions, was not reported.
Team name: Bruins. *Team mascot:* Bruin (costumed figure). *Colors:* Blue and gold. *Song:* "Sons of Westwood." *Conference:* Pac-10. *First intercollegiate football game:* 1919.
Coaches and their tenure: Terry Donahue (1982–95), Bob Toledo (1996–).
Athletic directors and their tenure: Bob Fischer (1982), Peter Dalis (1983–).

UCLA's mascot Bruin

UNIVERSITY OF CENTRAL FLORIDA
Orlando, Florida

Citrus Bowl (1936)

Originally known as the Tangerine Bowl, the stadium's name was changed to the Citrus Bowl in the 1980s. UCF played its first home game here in 1979. *Lights:* Yes. *Seating capacity:* 70,188. *Location:* Off campus. *Playing surface:* Grass. *Special features:* 5,000-sq. ft. conference center, 30 private suites, press box seating 250 journalists. *Other uses:* Citrus Bowl game played here each New Year's Day, annual All-Star Gridiron Classic game, soccer games, rock concerts, and motorcross races.

Original construction: 1936, at a cost of $115,000. *Additions and renovations:* In 1952 seating capacity was increased by 2,000. In 1968 5,000 seats were added and a press box was erected. Still another 33,000 seats were added in 1976. The latest seating capacity increase came in 1989, when 9,000 seats were added in each of the upper decks. Two escalator towers and Americans with Disabilities Act enhancements were added in 1999. Cost of the 1989 improvements was $30 million, with $9 million spent on the 1999 improvements. Revenue from the Orange County Tourist Development tax paid for these improvements.

Team name: Golden Knights. *Team mascot:* Knightro. *Colors:* Black and gold. *Song:* "UCF Fight Song." *Conference:* Independent. *First intercollegiate football game:* 1979.

Coaches and their tenure: Don Jones (1979–81), Sam Weir (1982), Lou Saban (1983), Jerry Anderson (1984), Gene McDowell (1985–97), Mike Kruczek (1998–).

Athletic directors and their tenure: Jack O'Leary (1979–81), Bill Peterson (1982–84), Gene McDowell (1985–93), Steve Sloan (1994–).

Knightro

CENTRAL MICHIGAN UNIVERSITY
Mt. Pleasant, Michigan

Kelly-Shorts Stadium (1972)

The stadium was named for former head football coach Bill Kelly and CMU alumnus Perry Shorts.

Lights: No. *Seating capacity:* 30,199. *Location:* On campus. *Playing surface:* Astroturf. *Special features:* Two-tier press box with guest suites on first level. *Other uses:* Field hockey games, Special Olympics.
Original construction: 1972, at cost of $2.2 million. *Renovations and additions:* In 1997–98 the home team locker room facility was expanded, an Indoor Athletic Complex was constructed, and seating capacity was increased by 10,000. Total cost of these improvements was $28 million. Source of financing these improvements was revenue bonds and private donations. *Projected additions:* None planned.
Team name: Chippewas. *Mascot:* None. *Colors:* Maroon and gold. *Song:* "CMU Fight Song." *Conference:* Mid-American. *First intercollegiate football game:* 1896.
Coaches and their tenure: Roy Kramer (1972–77), Herb Denomedi (1978–93), Dick Flynn (1994–).
Athletic directors and their tenure: Ted Kjolhede (1973–84), Dave Keilitz (1985–94), Herb Denomedi (1995–).

Central Michigan University logo

UNIVERSITY OF CINCINNATI
Cincinnati, Ohio

Nippert Stadium (1924)

The sixth oldest stadium in college football still in use, named for James Gamble Nippert, grandfather of Jimmy Nippert, a Cincinnati player who died in 1924 from an injury sustained in a game with Miami University of Ohio. *Lights:* Yes. *Seating capacity:* 35,000. *Location:* On campus. *Playing surface:* Artificial turf. *Special features:* Three-tiered press box with luxury VIP entertaining area, scoreboard and message center, and strength and conditioning center. *Other uses:* ROTC drills, Special Olympics, Band of America competitions, recreation, and intramurals.

Original construction: 1924. *Renovations and additions:* Seating capacity was doubled to 24,000 in 1936, with 4,000 seats added in 1954. Two-phase stadium renovation in 1991-92 fortified structural condition, added 11,000 seats, and installed new lighting and scoreboard. Cost of this renovation and addition was $10.5 million. Source of its financing was revenue bonds and private donations. *Projected renovations:* None planned.

Team name: Bearcats. *Team mascot:* Bearcat. *Colors:* Red and black. *Song:* "Cheer Cincinnati." *Conference:* USA. *First intercollegiate football game:* 1888.

Coaches and their tenure: George McLaren (1924–26), George Babcock (1927–30), Dana King (1931–34), Russ Cohen (1935–37), Joe Meyer (1938–42), Ray Nolting (1945–48), Sid Gillman (1949–54), George Blackburn (1955–60), Homer Rice (1967–68), Ray Callahan (1969–72), Tony Mason (1973–76), Ralph Staub (1977–80), Mike Gottfried (1981–82), Watson Brown (1983), Dave Currey (1984–88), Tim Murphy (1989–93), Rick Minter (1994 –).

Athletic directors and their tenure: Boyd Chambers (1924–27), R. George Babcock (1928–32), Dana M. King (1933–36), Charles Milehan (1937–60), George Smith (1961–73), Handman Wahl (1974–76), Bill Jenike (1977–80), Mike McGee (1981–84), Carl Meyer (1985–88), Rick Taylor (1989–94), Gerald O'Dell (1995–97), Bob Goin (1998–).

The Bearcat

CLEMSON UNIVERSITY
Clemson, South Carolina

Clemson Memorial Stadium (1942)

Stadium is frequently described as "Death Valley," a name given it by an opposing team's coach whose team consistently lost to Clemson by large margins. *Lights:* Yes. *Seating capacity:* 81,473. *Location:* On campus. *Playing surface:* Grass. Special features of stadium: Locker rooms, strength training room, administrative offices, replay board in west end zone, luxury suites, and "The Hill," entrance used by Clemson players prior to each home game. *Other uses:* Occasional concerts.
Original construction: $125,000. *Additions and renovations:* In 1958 18,000 sideline seats were added. Two years later seating capacity was increased to 53,000. In 1977-78 upper deck was expanded and in 1983 another addition brought seating capacity to its present figure. Cost of the 1983 addition was $13.5 million. Cost of other additions was not reported. All additions were financed by private donations. *Projected renovations:* Locker rooms, restrooms, training room, and concession areas will be renovated and year-round restaurant is planned for completion by 2003 at an estimated cost of $30 million. Private donations will be used to finance these improvements.
Team name: Tigers. *Team mascot:* Tiger (costumed figure). *Colors:* Northwest purple and burnt orange. *Song:* "Tiger Rag." *Conference:* Atlantic Coast. *First intercollegiate football game:* 1896.
Coaches and their tenure: Frank Howard (1942–69), Hootie Ingram (1970–72), Red Parker (1973–76), Charley Pell (1977–78), Danny Ford (1979–89), Ken Hatfield (1990–93), Tommy West (1994–98), Tommy Bowden (1999–).
Athletic directors and their tenure: Frank Howard (1942–71), Bill McClellan (1972–85), Bobby Robinson (1986–).

Above: Clemson Tiger. *Inset, left:* Logo for Clemson University.

UNIVERSITY OF COLORADO
Boulder, Colorado

Folsom Field (1924)

Named after Fred Folsom, the winningest coach in the University's first century.
Lights: No. *Seating capacity:* 52,005. *Location:* On campus. *Playing surface:* Grass. *Special features:* The Dal Ward Athletic Center at the north end houses all aspects of the football program. Spectators seated on the east side have spectacular mountain views. *Other uses:* Graduation exercises, concerts, Fourth of July celebration, intramural and club sports, conditioning.
Original construction: 1923, at a cost of $65,000. *Additions and renovations:* Additional seating has been provided on several occasions, most notably in 1956, 1967, and 1976. In 1976 wooden bleacher seats were removed and replaced with silver and gold aluminum bleachers, expanding the stadium to its present capacity. Cost of the 1967 renovation was $277,355. Cost of the other two renovations was not reported, nor was the source of financing.
Team name: Buffaloes. *Team mascot:* Ralphie IV, a live buffalo. *Colors:* Silver, gold and black. *Song:* "Fight CU." *Conference:* Big 12. *First intercollegiate football game:* 1890.
Coaches and their tenure:
Fred Folsom (1895–99, 1901-02, 1908–15), Myron Witham (1924–31), William Saunders (1932–34), Bunnie Oakes (1935–39), Frank Potts (1940), Jim Yeager (1941–43), Frank Potts (1944–45), Jim Yeager (1946–47), Dallas Ward (1948–58), Sonny Grandelius (1959–61), Bud Davis (1962), Eddie Crowder (1963–73), Bill Mallory (1974–78), Chuck Fairbanks (1979–81), Bill McCartney (1982–94), Bill Neuheisel (1995–98), Gary Barnett (1999–).
Athletic directors and their tenure: Harry Carlson (1924–65), Eddie Crowder (1966–84), Bill Marolt (1985–96), Dick Tharp (1997–).

Ralphie III, University of Colorado mascot

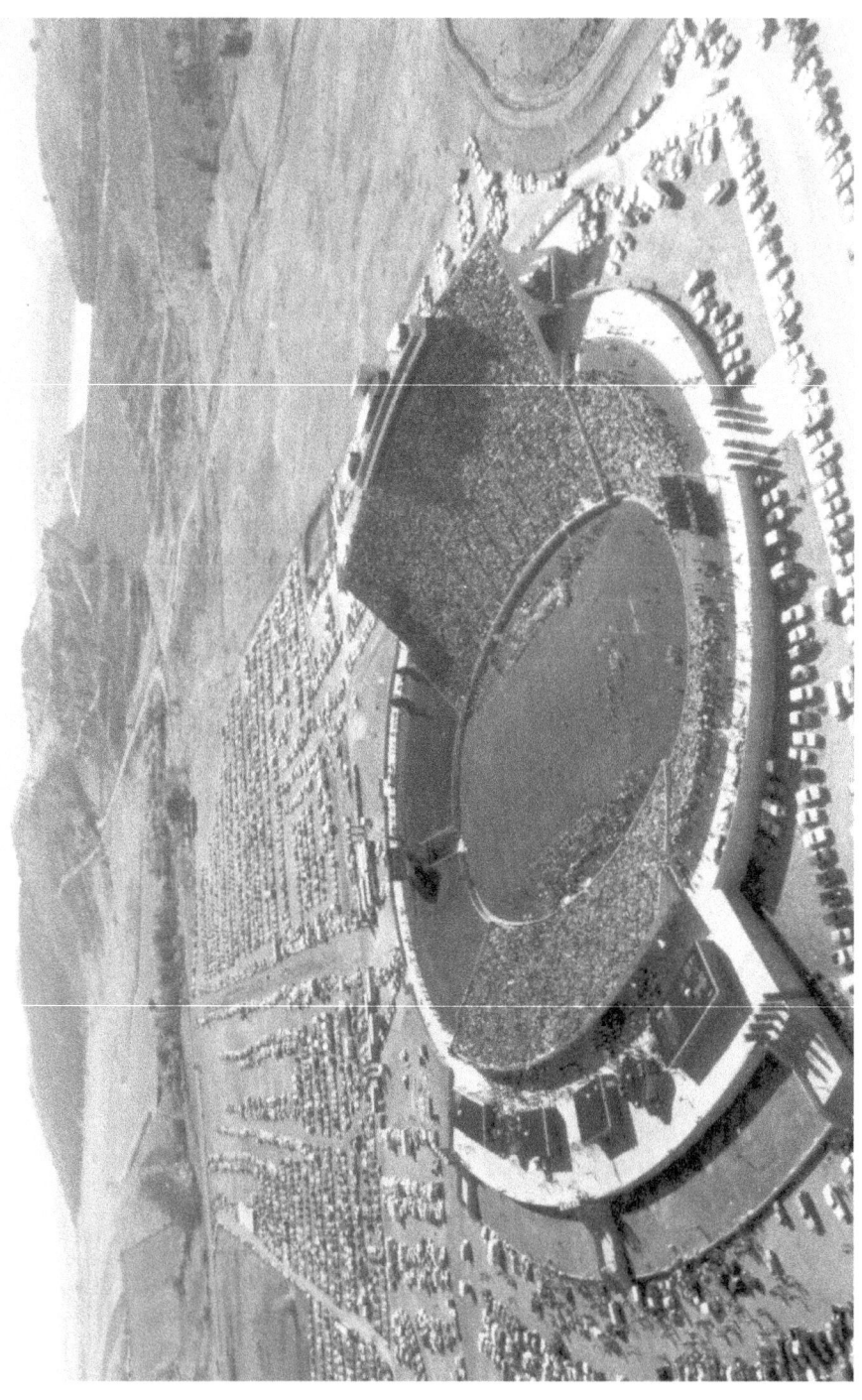

COLORADO STATE UNIVERSITY
Fort Collins, Colorado

Hughes Stadium (1968)

Named for former head football coach Harry Hughes, who held this position at CSU during the period 1911–41.
Lights: No. **Seating capacity:** 30,000. **Location:** Off campus. **Playing surface:** Grass. **Special features:** Locker rooms, press box, luxury suites. **Other uses:** Community activities such as marching band competitions.
Original construction: 1968, at a cost of $3 million. **Additions and renovations:** None. **Projected additions:** Plans are being developed to expand seating capacity, enlarge the press box, improve the lighting system, and change the playing field surface, with 2004 as the target date for completion of these improvements. Neither estimated cost nor method of financing these improvements has been reported.
Team name: Rams. **Team mascot:** Cam the Ram (live ram and costumed student). **Colors:** Green and gold. **Song:** "Fight On You Stalwart Rams." **Conference:** Mountain West. **First intercollegiate football game:** 1893.
Coaches and their tenure: Mike Lude (1968–69), Jerry Wampfler (1970–72), Sark Arslanian (1973–81), Leon Fuller (1982–88), Earle Bruce (1989–92), Sonny Lubick (1993–).
Athletic directors and their tenure: Jim Williams (1968), Perry Moore (1969–74), Jack O'Leary (1975), Thurman "Fum" McGraw (1976–86), Oval Jaymes (1987–91), Corey Johnson (1992–93), Tom Jurich (1994–97), Tim Weiser (1998–).

Cam the Ram

DUKE UNIVERSITY
Durham, North Carolina

Wallace Wade Stadium (1929)

Named for Wallace Wade, Blue Devil head coach for 16 years who took the team to two Rose Bowls. For national security reasons the 1942 Rose Bowl was played in this stadium, with Oregon State defeating Duke 20–16.

Lights: Yes. *Seating capacity:* 33,941. *Location:* On campus. *Playing surface:* Grass. *Special features:* Locker rooms, press box, computerized scoreboard, aluminum bench seating, coaches' offices, and sports medicine center. *Other uses:* Commencement, concerts, track meets. In 1990 the stadium was the site of the NCAA track and field championships.

Original construction: 1929, at a cost of $4 million. *Additions and renovations:* New press box was erected in 1982. Six years later the William David Murray Building, a multi-purpose athletic facility, including a conference room and computer room, was dedicated. Cost of this building was $2.5 million. *Projected additions:* Currently the Schwartz-Butters Athletic Center is under construction on northwest side of stadium. This structure will include a Duke Sports Hall of Fame, Student-Athlete Academic Center, locker rooms equipped with jacuzzi and sauna, and weight-aerobic rooms. Completion of this building is expected in 2000. Cost of the facility was not reported. Revenue from fund-raising campaigns financed cost of all improvements.

Team name: Blue Devils. *Team mascot:* Blue Devil. *Colors:* Navy blue and white. *Song:* "Fight, Blue Devils, Fight." *Conference:* Atlantic Coast. *First intercollegiate football game:* 1888.

Coaches and their tenure: James Dehart (1929–30), Wallace Wade (1931–41), Eddie Cameron (1942–45), Wallace Wade (1946–50), Bill Murray (1951–65), Tom Harp (1966–70), Mike McGee (1971–78), Shirley "Red" Wilson (1979–82), Steve Sloan (1983–86), Steve Spurrier (1987–89), Barry Wilson (1990–93), Fred Goldsmith (1994–98), Carl Franks (1999–).

Athletic directors and their tenure: Eddie Cameron served as acting athletic director during the period 1942–50. There was no athletic director or acting athletic director from 1929–41. Eddie Cameron (1951–72), Carl James (1973–77), Tom Butters (1978–98), Joe Alleva (1999–).

Duke Blue Devil

EAST CAROLINA UNIVERSITY
Greenville, North Carolina

James S. Ficklen Stadium (1963)

In 1994 the stadium was renamed the Dowdy-Ficklen Stadium in honor of James S. Ficklen and Ron Dowdy. At that time Ficklen was a Greenville resident and leading tobacco executive and Dowdy, an ECU graduate, was a member of the ECU Board of Trustees.

Lights: Yes. **Seating capacity:** 43,000. **Location:** On campus. **Playing surface:** Grass. **Special features:** Three-level press box with elevator for access, modern scoreboard with lightbank message center. **Other uses:** Graduation exercises, one-time site for Franklin Graham Crusade.

Original construction: 1963, cost of $300,000. **Additions and renovations:** 1978 addition boosted seating capacity from 20,000 to 35,000. Addition of upper deck in 1997 increased this capacity to 43,000. Luxury suites were constructed in 1999 at a cost of $7 million. Cost of 1978 addition was $2.5 million, with cost of 1997 addition estimated at $13 million. Financing methods were private donations, fundraising drive, and state appropriations. **Projected additions:** None planned.

Team name: Pirates. **Team mascot:** Pirate. **Colors:** Purple and gold. **Song:** "ECU Fight Song." **Conference:** USA. **First intercollegiate football game:** 1932.

Coaches and their tenure: Clarence Stasavich (1963–69), Mike McGee (1970), Sonny Randle (1971–73), Pat Dye (1974–79), Ed Emory (1980–84), Art Baker (1985–88), Bill Lewis (1989–91), Steve Logan (1992–).

Athletic directors and their tenure: Clarence Stasavich (1963–75), Bill Cain (1976–80), Ken Karr (1981–87), Dave Hart, Jr. (1988–95), Mike Hamrick (1996–).

The ECU Pirate

EASTERN MICHIGAN UNIVERSITY
Ypsilanti, Michigan

Rynearson Stadium (1969)

Named for the late Elton J. Rynearson, Sr., head football coach at EMU for 26 seasons who ended his career in 1948. His teams compiled a record of 144–58–15.

Lights: Yes. **Seating capacity:** 30,200. **Location:** On campus. **Playing surface:** Astroturf. **Special features:** Two-level press box, with top level used as a hospitality area, locker rooms. **Other uses:** Local high schools football games, track meets, and drum corps competitions.

Original construction: 1969, at a cost of $1.4 million. University funds financed the cost of construction. **Additions and renovations:** In 1974 7,000 seats were added. Another 8,000 seats were added in 1992 to bring capacity to its current figure. Renovations in 1991–92 included the construction of a new team building, an expanded press box, installation of a state-of-the-art scoreboard, and refurbishing rest rooms and concession stands. Private donations financed the cost of these $13 million improvements.

Team name: Eagles. **Team mascot:** Eagle (costumed figure). **Colors:** Green and white. **Song:** "Eastern Eagles Fight Song." **Conference:** Mid-American. **First intercollegiate football game:** 1891.

Coaches and their tenure: Dan Boisture (1969–73), George Mans (1974–75), Ed Chlebek (1976–77), Mike Stock (1978–82), Jim Harkema (1983–92), Ron Cooper (1993–94), Rick Rasnick (1995–).

Athletic directors and their tenure: "Frosty" Ferzacca (1969–74), Albert Smith (1975–76), Ron Oestrike (1977), Alex Agase (1978–82), Paul Shoults (1983–85), Eugene Smith (1986–93), Tim Weiser (1994–98), David Diles (1999–).

Eastern Michigan University logo

UNIVERSITY OF FLORIDA
Gainesville, Florida

Ben Hill Griffin Stadium (1930)

Since 1989 the stadium has been named for Ben Hill Griffin, a life-long Gator supporter and University benefactor.

Lights: Yes. *Seating capacity:* 83,000. *Location:* On campus. *Special features:* Locker rooms, luxury suites, President's box, south end zone conference room, press box, athletic training center, skybox tower.

Playing surface: Natural grass. *Other uses:* Homecoming pep rally (Gator Growl), state high school football playoffs.

Original construction: 1930, cost not reported. *Additions and renovations:* In 1949–50 west stands were expanded, bringing seating capacity to 40,116; 10,000 seats were added to east side in 1965–66; in 1982 seating capacity was increased to 72,000, and in 1991 additional seating in north end zone brought capacity to its current figure. Video board was installed in 1998 at a cost of $2.1 million. Cost of 1991 addition was $17 million. Booster fund-raising campaigns and Athletic Department funds financed all additions.

Team name: Gators. *Team mascot:* Albert the Alligator. *Colors:* Orange and blue. *Song:* "The Orange and Blue." *Conference:* Southeastern. *First intercollegiate football game:* 1906.

Coaches and their tenure: Charles Bachman (1930–32), D.K. "Dutch" Stanley (1933–35), Josh Cody (1936–39), Tom Lieb (1940–45), Ray "Bear" Wolf (1946–49), Bob Woodruff (1950–59), Ray Graves (1960–69), Doug Dickey (1970–78), Charles Pell (1979–84), Galen Hall (1985–89), Steve Spurrier (1990–).

Athletic directors and their tenure: Edgar Charles Jones (1930–36), Josh Cody (1937–40), Percy Beard (1941–47), R.B. Wolf (1948–50), Bob Woodruff (1951–60), Ray Graves (1961–79), Bill Carr (1980–86), Bill Arnsparger (1987–92), Jeremy N. Foley (1993 —).

University of Florida Gator logo

FLORIDA STATE UNIVERSITY
Tallahassee, Florida

Doak S. Campbell Stadium (1950)

Named for Doak S. Campbell, a former University president.

Lights: Yes. *Seating capacity:* 80,000. *Location:* On campus. *Playing surface:* Grass. *Special features:* Locker rooms, press box, luxury suites, full restaurant and food court, and the University Center, a complex of administrative and student offices surrounding the stadium. *Other uses:* None.

Original construction: 1950, cost not reported. *Additions and renovations:* Since the stadium opened nine expansions in seating capacity have been made, with the latest occurring in 1997. That same year 70 sky boxes were added and a new three-level press box was constructed. Cost of these improvements was not reported. They were financed through private funds provided by the Seminole Boosters, a support group for FSU athletic programs.

Team name: Seminoles. *Team mascot:* Chief Osceola and Renegade, his horse. *Colors:* Garnet and gold. *Song:* "FSU Fight Song." *Conference:* Atlantic Coast. *First intercollegiate football game:* 1947.

Coaches and their tenure: Don Vellen (1950–52), Tom Nugent (1953–58), Perry Moss (1959), Bill Peterson (1960–70), Larry Jones (1971–73), Darrell Mudva (1974–75), Bobby Bowden (1976–).

Athletic directors and their tenure: Dr. Howard Danforth (1950–56), Tom Nugent (1957–58), Perry Moss (1959), Vaughn Marche (1960–70), Clay Stapleton (1971–72), John Bridgers (1973–79), Hootie Ingram (1980–89), Bob Goin (1990–94), Dave Hart (1995–).

Chief Osceola and Renegade

FRESNO STATE UNIVERSITY
Fresno, California

Bulldog Stadium (1980)

The stadium is named for a bulldog, the school mascot.

Lights: Yes. A unique cantilevered system extends toward the field and is directed downward to the field. *Seating capacity:* 41,031. *Location:* Off campus. *Playing field surface:* Grass. *Special features:* 22 sky suites with seating for 20.

Original construction: 1979; $7 million was obtained from a local fund-raising campaign. *Renovations and additions:* In 1991 10,000 additional seats were installed by filling in panels beyond the north and south end zones with bench seating and a reconfiguration of seating on the stadium's east side. Sky suites were completed in 1992. Cost of this addition was not reported. *Other uses:* Soccer games, commencement exercises. *Projected additions:* None planned.

Team name: Bulldogs. *Team mascot:* Bulldog. *Colors:* Cardinal and blue. *Song:* "Bulldog Fight Song." *Conference:* Western Athletic. *First intercollegiate football game:* 1921.

Coaches and their tenure: Arthur Jones (1921–28), Stan Borleske (1929–32), Leo Harris (1933–35), Jimmy Bradshaw (1936–42), Earl Wright (1944), Alvin Pearson (1945–46), Ken Gleason (1947–48), Duke Jacobs (1950–51), Clark Van Galder (1952–58), Cecil Coleman (1959–63), Phil Krueger (1964– 65), Darryl Rogers (1966–72), J.R. Boone (1973–75), Bob Padilla (1978–79), Jim Sweeney (1976–77, 1980–96), Pat Hill (1997–).

Athletic directors and their tenure: None prior to 1981. Russ Sloan (1981–84), Jack Lengyel (1985–87), Dr. Gary A. Cunningham (1988–96), Dr. Allen R. Bohl (1997–).

Logo for Fresno State Bulldogs

UNIVERSITY OF GEORGIA
Athens, Georgia

Sanford Stadium (1929)

Named for Steadman V. Sanford, former chairman of the Faculty Athletic Committee, UGA president, and ex-chancellor of the University System of Georgia.

Lights: Yes. **Seating capacity:** 86,117. **Location:** On campus. **Playing surface:** Natural grass. **Special features:** Locker rooms, weight room, training room, player lounge, and press box. West end of stadium is burial place of four bulldogs who were team mascots. **Other uses:** For six days in the summer of 1996 the stadium hosted the medal round of men's and women's soccer in the Centennial Olympic Games, with a sellout crowd for the men's championship game.

Original construction: 1929, at a cost of $360,000. **Additions and renovations:** Additional seats were erected in 1949, 1964, 1967, 1981, and 1991. New lights were installed in 1982. In 1984 the Lettermen's Club with a large dining/meeting room was added to the east end. A decade later double deck luxury sky suites were built atop the south side upper deck. Cost of all these improvements was $25 million. The method of financing them was not reported.

Team name: Bulldogs. **Team mascot:** UGA V (bulldog). **Colors:** Red and black. **Song:** "Glory, Glory." **Conference:** Southeastern. **First intercollegiate football game:** 1892.

Coaches and their tenure: Harry Mehre (1929–37), Joel Hunt (1938), Wally Butts (1939–60), Johnny Griffith (1961–63), Vince Dooley (1964–88), Ray Goff (1989–95), Jim Donnan (1996–).

Athletic directors and their tenure: Herman J. Stegeman (1929–38), Wally Butts (1939–62), Joel Eaves (1963–78), Vince Dooley (1979–).

UGA V

GEORGIA INSTITUTE OF TECHNOLOGY
Atlanta, Georgia

Bobby Dodd Stadium, formerly Grant Field (1913)

Named for Bobby Dodd, head football coach at Georgia Tech (1945–66) who led the Yellow Jackets to 13 bowl games. In 1988 the stadium was renamed Bobby Dodd Stadium.

Lights: Yes. **Seating capacity:** 46,000. **Location:** On campus. **Playing surface:** Natural grass. **Special features:** Press box, scoreboards with video capability. Stadium is the oldest of any team in NCAA Division I-A. **Other uses:** None.

Original construction: 1913, cost not reported. **Additions and renovations:** In 1924 the addition of concrete stands brought seating capacity to 18,000. This figure was expanded to 40,000 in 1948. Seating capacity reached 53,000 in 1962 with the addition of a second deck to the east side of the stadium. Five years later double-decking of the west side increased the capacity to 58,121. In 1986 the south stands were demolished, lowering the seating capacity to 46,000 to make way for the William C. Wardlaw Center, completed in 1988. Four years later the Bill Moore Student Success Center was built. This facility houses Tech's admissions, student recruiting, and student financial services offices. In 1992, 32 enclosed executive suites were added to the west stands and the President's Suite was expanded. Neither the cost nor method of financing these additions was reported.

Team name: Yellow Jackets and Rambling Wreck. **Team mascot:** Buzz (costumed wasp). **Colors:** Old gold and white. **Song:** "The Rambling Wreck Fight Song." **Conference:** Atlantic Coast. **First intercollegiate football game:** 1892.

Coaches and their tenure: John Heisman (1913–19), William Alexander (1920–44), Bobby Dodd (1945–66), Bud Carson (1967–71), Bill Fulcher (1972–73), Pepper Rodgers (1974–79), Bill Curry (1980–86), Bobby Ross (1987–91), Bill Lewis (1992–94), George O'Leary (1995–).

Athletic directors and their tenure: John Heisman (l913–19), William Alexander (1920–50), Bobby Dodd (1951–76), Doug Weaver (1977–79), Homer Rice (1980–96), Dave Braine (1997–).

Buzz

UNIVERSITY OF HAWAII
Honolulu, Hawaii

Aloha Stadium (1975)

Lights: Yes. *Seating capacity:* 50,000. *Location:* Off campus. *Playing field surface:* Astroturf. *Special features:* Four locker rooms with training rooms, press rooms, and offices for coaches, trainers, and physicians. Special configuration enables stadium to be used for baseball as well as football. *Other uses:* Baseball and soccer games, flea market, and entertainment events such as concerts, tractor pulls, and motorcross races.

Original construction: 1975, cost of $27 million. *Additions and renovations:* None. Issuance of general obligation bonds was method used to finance cost of original construction. *Projected additions:* None planned.

Team name: Rainbow Warriors. *Mascot:* Rainbow Warrior. *Colors:* Green and white. *Song:* "Co-ed." *Conference:* Western Athletic. *First intercollegiate football game:* 1920.

Coaches and their tenure: Larry Price (1975–76), Dick Tomey (1977–86), Bob Wagner (1987–95), Fred von Appen (1996–98), June Jones (1999–).

Athletic directors and their tenure: Dr. Edward Chui (1975), Ray Nagel (1976–83), Stan Sheriff (1984–93), Hugh Yoshida (1994–).

The Rainbow Warrior from University of Hawaii

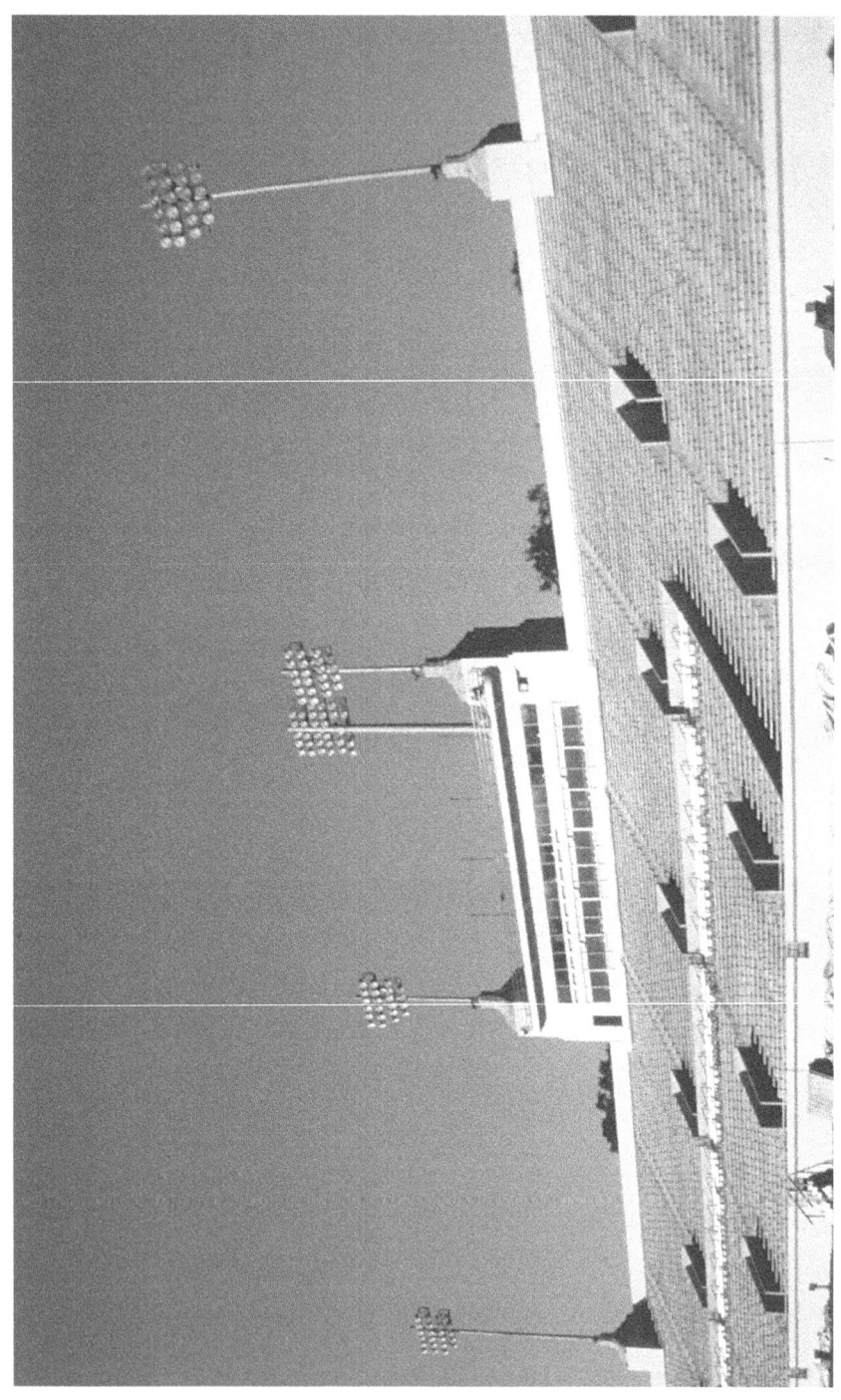

UNIVERSITY OF HOUSTON
Houston, Texas

Robertson Stadium (1937)

Named for Corby Robertson, a University board of regents member, chairman of the Board's athletics committee, and a major benefactor of the University. During the period 1937–45 Houston high school teams used the stadium.

Lights: Yes. **Seating capacity:** 33,000. **Location:** On campus. **Playing surface:** Grass. **Special features:** Locker rooms, coaches' offices, press box, 30 luxury suites. **Other uses:** Commencement exercises, concerts, soccer games, and track meets.

Original construction: 1937, at a cost of $1.3 million. **Additions and renovations:** Added 20 luxury boxes in 1998. The following year 13,000 seats were added, bringing seating capacity to its current figure. Cost of the additional seats was $7 million, with private gifts financing this cost.

Team name: Cougars. **Team mascot:** Cougar (costumed figure, not a live animal). **Colors:** Red and white. **Song:** "On to Glory." **Conference:** USA. **First intercollegiate football game:** 1946.

Coaches and their tenure: Jewell Wallace (1946–47), Clyde Lee (1948–54), Bill Meek (1955–56), Harold Lahar (1957–61), Bill Yeoman (1962–86), Jack Pardee (1987–89), John Jenkins (1990–92), Kim Helton (1993–).

Athletic directors and their tenure: Harry Fouke (1946–79), Cedric Dempsey (1980–82), John Kasser (1983–84), Tom Ford (1985–86), Rudy Davalos (1987–92), Bill Carr (1993–97), Chet Gladchuk (1998–).

UNIVERSITY OF IDAHO
Moscow, Idaho

Kibbie Dome (1975)

Named for William H. Kibbie, deceased University of Idaho alumnus and benefactor.

Lights: Yes. *Seating capacity:* 16,000 (smallest seating capacity among the 114 NCAA Division I-A teams). *Location:* On campus. *Playing surface:* Astroturf. *Special features:* Locker rooms, coaches' offices, weight facility. *Other uses:* Basketball games, track meets.

Original construction: 1975, at a cost of $4 million. Financing was done with the support of the Vandal Boosters, an alumni fund-raising group. *Additions and renovations:* None. *Projected additions:* Academic support services for athletes and enlargement of weight room and training facilities will be completed by 2005. These improvements will be financed through support from the Vandal Boosters.

Team name: Vandals. *Team mascot:* Joe Vandal (costumed figure). *Colors:* Black, gold, and silver. *Song:* "Go Vandals Go." *Conference:* Big West. *First intercollegiate football game:* 1894.

Coaches and their tenure: Ed Troxel (1975–77), Jerry Davitch (1978–81), Dennis Erickson (1982–85), Keith Gilbertson (1986–88), John L. Smith (1989–94), Chris Tormey (1995–).

Athletic directors and their tenure: Dr. Leon Green (1975–77), Bill Belknap (1978–88), Gary Hunter (1989–92), Pete Liske (1993–95), Jaymes Oval (1996–98), Mike Bohn (1999–).

Joe Vandal

University of Illinois
Urbana-Champaign, Illinois

Memorial Stadium (1924)

Stadium was named in memory of University alumni who died in World War I.

Lights: Yes. *Seating capacity:* 70,904. *Location:* On campus. *Playing surface:* Artificial turf. *Special features:* 100 pillars — 50 on each side — are located in balconies, with one dedicated to each Illinois soldier who died in World War I. *Other uses:* Occasional campus-wide meetings.

Original construction: 1921–24. *Renovations and additions:* In 1992 all concrete stands and bleachers were replaced with brand new concrete structures at a cost of $18 million. Cost of original construction was $1.7 million. Student bond issuance paid for original construction. Student activity fees and debt service financed renovation cost. No further addition or renovation is planned.

Team name: Fighting Illini. *Team mascot:* Chief Illiniwek (a symbol, not a mascot). *Colors:* Orange and blue. *Song:* "Illinois Loyalty." *Conference:* Big Ten. First *intercollegiate football game:* 1890.

Head coaches and their tenure: Bob Zuppke (1924–41), Ray Eliot (1942–59), Pete Elliott (1960–66), Jim Valek (1967–70), Bob Blackman (1971–76), Gary Moeller (1977–79), Mike White (1980–87), John Mackovic (1988–91), Lou Tepper (1992–96), Ron Turner (1997–).

Athletic directors and their tenure: George Huff (1924–36), Wendell Wilson (1937–41), Douglas Mills (1942–66), Gene Vance (1967–71), Cecil Coleman (1972–79), Neale Stoner (1980–88), John Mackovic (1988–91), Ron Guenther (1992–).

Chief Illiniwek

Indiana University
Bloomington, Indiana

Memorial Stadium (1960)

Lights: Yes. **Seating capacity:** 52,000. **Location:** On campus. **Playing surface:** Grass. **Special features:** No unique features. **Other uses:** Graduation ceremonies, concerts.

Original construction: 1958. **Additions and renovations:** Installation of Astroturf in 1971 and of new grass field in 1998. No seating additions since stadium was built. Cost of original construction not reported. Method of financing this cost not reported. No future additions or renovations are planned.

Team name: Hoosiers. **Team mascot:** None. **Colors:** Cream and crimson. **Song:** "Indiana, Our Indiana." **Conference:** Big Ten. **First intercollegiate football game:** 1887.

Head coaches and their tenure: Phil Dickens (1960–64), John Pont (1965–72), Lee Corso (1973–82), Sam Wyche (1983), Bill Mallory (1984–96), Cam Cameron (1997–).

Athletic directors and their tenure: Frank Allen (1960–61), Bill Orwig (1962–75), Paul Dietzel (1976–78), Ralph Floyd (1979–90), Ed Williams (1991), Clarence Doninger (1992–).

Indiana University logo

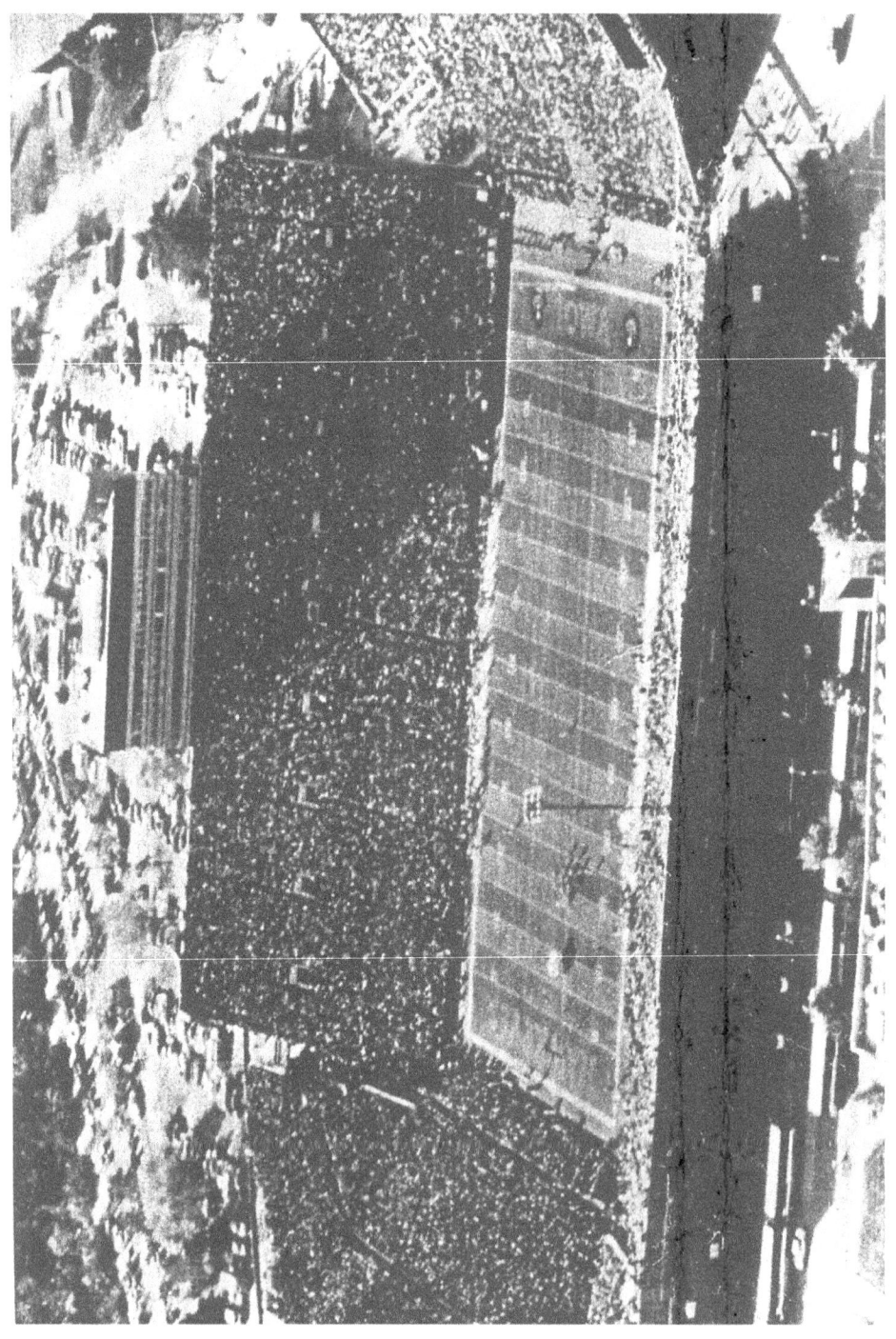

UNIVERSITY OF IOWA
Iowa City, Iowa

Kinnick Stadium (1929)

Named after Nile Kinnick, a tailback on the UI team and winner of the Heisman Trophy in 1939.
Lights: No. **Seating capacity:** 70,397. **Location:** On campus. **Playing surface:** Grass. **Special features:** Sony Jumbotron with video display, state-of-the-art scoreboard. **Other uses:** None.
Original construction: 1929, at a cost of $497,151. **Additions and renovations:** In 1958 a five-floor press box was constructed at a cost of $490,600. This box was completely refurbished in 1995, when 18 luxury suites were built. Cost of the 1995 renovation was $3 million. Cost of the 1958 construction was not reported. Athletic Department funds and private donations were used to finance the 1995 renovation.
Team name: Hawkeyes. **Team mascot:** Herky. **Colors:** Old gold and black. **Song:** "Iowa Fight Song." **Conference:** Big Ten. **First intercollegiate football game:** 1889.
Coaches and their tenure: Burg Ingwersen (1929–31), Ossie Solem (1932–36), Irl Tubbs (1937–38), Eddie Anderson (1939–42), Slip Madigan (1943–44), Clem Crowe (1945), Eddie Anderson (1946–49), Leonard Raffensperger (1950–51), Forest Evashevski (1952–60), Jerry Burns (1961–65), Ray Nagel (1966–70), Frank X. Lauterbur (1971–73), Bob Cummings (1974–78), Hayden Fry (1979–98), Kirk Ferentz (1999–).
Athletic directors and their tenure: Edward Lauer (1929–34), Ossie Solem (1935–36), Ernest G. Schroeder (1937–47), Paul W. Brechler (1948–60), Forest Evasheveski (1961–70), Chalmers (Bump) Elliott (1971–91), Robert A. Bowlsby (1992–).

Herky

IOWA STATE UNIVERSITY
Ames, Iowa

Jack Trice Stadium (1975)

Named after Jack Trice, the first African-American athlete at Iowa State. Trice played on the 1922 and 1923 football teams and tragically died as a result of a lung condition a few days following the Iowa State–Minnesota game in October 1923. Known as Cyclone Stadium until 1997, the stadium was renamed in 1997 in memory of Trice.

Lights: No. *Seating capacity:* 43,000. *Location:* Off campus. *Playing surface:* Grass. *Special features:* 23 luxury units, football equipment unit, state-of-the-art scoreboard, locker rooms. *Other uses:* Occasional concerts, Farm Aid Concert was held here in 1989.

Original construction: 1973, at an estimated cost of $7.6 million. *Additions and renovations:* End zone bleachers were added in 1976. In 1994 a new scoreboard was installed. Two years later the $10.6 million Jacobson Building was constructed. This building includes a football office complex, expanded strength and conditioning work areas, comprehensive sports medicine center, a 140-seat auditorium for team meetings, and a video production office. In 1997 a $6.2 million three-level press tower was added. Two fields — a natural grass practice field and an artificial turf field — were opened near the stadium in 1999 at an estimated cost of $1.2 million. All improvements were financed by private donations.

Team name: Cyclones. *Team mascot:* "Cy" the cardinal. *Colors:* Cardinal and gold. *Song:* "ISU Fights." *Conference:* Big 12. *First intercollegiate football game:* 1892.

Coaches and their tenure: Earle Bruce (1975–78), Donnie Duncan (1979–82), Jim Criner (1983–86), Jim Walden (1987–94), Dan McCarney (1995–).

Athletic directors and their tenure: Lou McCullough (1975–83), Max Urick (1984–93), Gene Smith (1994–).

Cy the Cardinal

UNIVERSITY OF KANSAS
Lawrence, Kansas

Kansas Memorial Stadium (1921)

Named in memory of UK students who died in World War I. Stadium was the first such structure built on a college campus west of the Mississippi River.

Lights: Yes. **Seating capacity:** 50,250. **Location:** On campus. **Playing surface:** Astroturf. **Special features:** Locker rooms, press box. **Other uses:** Track meets, including Kansas Relays, numerous community and musical activities.

Original construction: 1921, at a cost exceeding $200,000 secured from faculty and student pledges in a three-day period. **Additions and renovations:** In 1927 the seating capacity was increased to 35,000 with an extension of east and west sections to the south. In 1963 a new press box was constructed and 10,000 seats were added. Wooden seats were replaced with aluminum bleachers and new dressing and training rooms were built in 1978. Another 6,000 seats were added in 1992. During 1998-99 concession stands and restrooms were upgraded and the press box was expanded. Cost of the latest improvements was $25 million. Method of financing additions and renovations was not reported.

Team name: Jayhawks. **Team mascot:** Jayhawk (costumed figure). **Colors:** Crimson and blue. **Song:** "I'm a Jayhawk." **Conference:** Big 12. **First intercollegiate football game:** 1890.

Coaches and their tenure: Potsy Clark (1921–25), Frank Cappon (1926–27), Bill Hargiss (1928–32), Add Lindsey (1932–38), Gwinn Henry (1939–42), Henry Shank (1943–45), George Sauer (1946–47), J.V. Sikes (1948–53), Chuck Mather (1954–57), Jack Mitchell (1958–66), Pepper Rodgers (1967–70), Don Fambrough (1971–74), Bud Moore (1975–78), Don Fambrough (1979–82), Mike Gottfried (1983–85), Bob Valesente (1986–87), Glen Mason (1988–96), Terry Allen (1997–).

Athletic directors and their tenure: Dr. F.C. "Phog" Allen (1921–37), Gwinn Henry (1938–42), Karl Klooz (1943), E.C. Quigley (1944–49), Arthur "Dutch" Lonborg (1950–63), Wade R. Stinson (1964–72), Clyde Walker (1973–77), Bob Marcum (1978–81), Jim Lessig (1982), Monte Johnson (1983–86), Dr. Bob Frederick (1987–).

Jayhawk

UNIVERSITY OF KANSAS
Lawrence, Kansas

Kansas Memorial Stadium (1921)

Named in memory of UK students who died in World War I. Stadium was the first such structure built on a college campus west of the Mississippi River.

Lights: Yes. *Seating capacity:* 50,250. *Location:* On campus. *Playing surface:* Astroturf. *Special features:* Locker rooms, press box. *Other uses:* Track meets, including Kansas Relays, numerous community and musical activities.

Original construction: 1921, at a cost exceeding $200,000 secured from faculty and student pledges in a three-day period. *Additions and renovations:* In 1927 the seating capacity was increased to 35,000 with an extension of east and west sections to the south. In 1963 a new press box was constructed and 10,000 seats were added. Wooden seats were replaced with aluminum bleachers and new dressing and training rooms were built in 1978. Another 6,000 seats were added in 1992. During 1998-99 concession stands and restrooms were upgraded and the press box was expanded. Cost of the latest improvements was $25 million. Method of financing additions and renovations was not reported.

Team name: Jayhawks. *Team mascot:* Jayhawk (costumed figure). *Colors:* Crimson and blue. *Song:* "I'm a Jayhawk." *Conference:* Big 12. *First intercollegiate football game:* 1890.

Coaches and their tenure: Potsy Clark (1921–25), Frank Cappon (1926–27), Bill Hargiss (1928–32), Add Lindsey (1932–38), Gwinn Henry (1939–42), Henry Shank (1943–45), George Sauer (1946–47), J.V. Sikes (1948–53), Chuck Mather (1954–57), Jack Mitchell (1958–66), Pepper Rodgers (1967–70), Don Fambrough (1971–74), Bud Moore (1975–78), Don Fambrough (1979–82), Mike Gottfried (1983–85), Bob Valesente (1986–87), Glen Mason (1988–96), Terry Allen (1997–).

Athletic directors and their tenure: Dr. F.C. "Phog" Allen (1921–37), Gwinn Henry (1938–42), Karl Klooz (1943), E.C. Quigley (1944–49), Arthur "Dutch" Lonborg (1950–63), Wade R. Stinson (1964–72), Clyde Walker (1973–77), Bob Marcum (1978–81), Jim Lessig (1982), Monte Johnson (1983–86), Dr. Bob Frederick (1987–).

Jayhawk

KANSAS STATE UNIVERSITY
Manhattan, Kansas

KSU Stadium (1968)

Lights: Yes. **Seating capacity:** 42,000. **Location:** On campus. **Playing surface:** Astroturf. **Special features:** 54 sky suites, football complex consisting of weight room, training facility, locker rooms, coaches' offices, and an academic learning center. **Other uses:** None.

Original construction: 1968, at a cost of $1.6 million. **Additions and renovations:** In 1999 the stadium was enlarged by 8,000 seats and 31 sky suites were added. Cost of these additions was $12.8 million. This cost was financed by the issuance of bonds and revenue from the sale of tickets for premium seating.

Team name: Wildcats. **Team mascot:** Willie the Wildcat. **Colors:** Purple and white. **Song:** "Wildcat Victory." **Conference:** Big 12. **First intercollegiate football game:** 1896.

Coaches and their tenure: Vince Gibson (1968–74), Ellis Rainsberger (1975–77), Jim Dickey (1978–85), Stan Parrish (1986–88), Bill Snyder (1989–).

Athletic directors and their tenure: Ernie Barrett (1968–75), John "Jersey" Jermier (1976–77), Deloss Dodds (1978–81), Dick Towers (1982–85), Larry Travis (1986–88), Steve Miller (1989–91), Milt Richards (1992–93), Max Urick (1994–).

Willie the Wildcat

KENT STATE UNIVERSITY
Kent, Ohio

Dix Stadium (1970)

Named for Robert C. Dix, a member of the Kent State Board of Trustees for more than three decades.

Lights: Yes. **Seating capacity:** 30,520. **Location:** On campus. **Playing surface:** Artificial turf. **Special features:** Locker rooms, press box. **Other uses:** High school football games, commencement exercises.

Original construction: 1969, at a cost of $5.3 million. **Additions and renovations:** Lights were installed on field in 1996, artificial turf was laid on field in 1997, and scoreboard was installed in 1998. Cost of these renovations was not reported. **Projected additions:** Addition of east side bleachers, renovation of locker rooms, equipment room, and training room, with no target date set for completion of these improvements. Their combined projected cost is $3 million. University funds and private donations will be used to finance this cost.

Team name: Golden Flashes. **Team mascot:** Golden eagle. **Colors:** Navy blue and gold. **Song:** Not reported. **Conference:** Mid-American. **First intercollegiate football game:** 1920.

Coaches and their tenure: Dave Puddington (1970), Don James (1971–74), Dennis Fitzgerald (1975–77), Ron Blackledge (1978–80), Ed Chlebek (1981–82), Dick Scesniak (1983–85), Glen Mason (1986–87), Dick Crum (1988–90), Pete Cordelli (1991–93), Jim Corrigall (1994–97), Dean Pees (1998–).

Athletic directors and their tenure: Mike Lude (1970–76), Don Dufek (1977–80), Paul Amodio (1981–93), Laing Kennedy (1994–).

Golden Eagle

UNIVERSITY OF KENTUCKY
Lexington, Kentucky

Commonwealth Stadium (1973)

Lights: Yes. *Seating capacity:* 68,000. *Location:* On campus. *Playing surface:* Grass. *Special features:* Press box, locker rooms, 40 luxury suites. *Other uses:* None.

Original construction: 1973, at a cost of $12 million. *Additions and renovations:* Both ends of stadium were enclosed and seating capacity increased by 12,000 in 1999. In the same year 40 luxury suites were built, ten in each corner of the stadium. Cost of these improvements was $24 million. Funds from the University Athletic Department were used to finance the improvements.

Team name: Wildcats. *Team mascot:* Wildcat (costumed student). *Colors:* Blue and white. *Song:* "On, On U. of K." *Conference:* Southeastern. *First intercollegiate football game:* 1880.

Coaches and their tenure: Fran Curci (1973–81), Jerry Claiborne (1982–89), Bill Curry (1990–96), Hal Mumme (1997–).

Athletic directors and their tenure: Harry Lancaster (1973–75), Cliff Hagan (1976–89), C.M. Newton (1990–).

Wildcat of the University of Kentucky

LOUISIANA STATE UNIVERSITY
Baton Rouge, Louisiana

Tiger Stadium (1924)

Lights: Yes. *Seating capacity:* 80,000. *Location:* On campus. *Playing surface:* Grass. *Special features:* Press box, once served as a dormitory for about 1,500 students. *Other uses:* None.

Original construction: 1924, cost not reported. *Additions and renovations:* 10,000 seats were added in 1928. In 1936 24,000 seats were added to the north end, creating a horseshoe configuration. This horseshoe was turned into a bowl in 1953, when seating capacity was increased to 67,720. In 1978 an addition raised seating capacity to 78,000. Seven years later 25,000 chairback seats were added to replace older "bench" type seats. Revenue generated from the sale of luxury suites has helped to finance these additions, the cost of which was not reported. *Projected additions:* By the fall of 2000 11,000 additional seats will be in place and 70 skyboxes will be available for use. Cost of this addition was not estimated.

Team name: Tigers. *Team mascot:* Tiger (costumed figure). *Colors:* Purple and gold. *Song:* "LSU Fight Song." *Conference:* Southeastern. *First intercollegiate football game:* 1893.

Coaches and their tenure: Coaches for 1924–32 period were not available. L.M. "Biff" Jones (1933–34), Bernie Moore (1935–47), Gaynell Tinsley (1948–54), Paul Dietzel (1955–61), Charlie McClendon (1962–79), Jerry Stovall (1980–83), Bill Arnsparger (1984–86), Mike Archer (1987–90), Curley Hallman (1991–94), Gerry DiNardo (1995–99), Nick Saban (2000–).

Athletic directors and their tenure: Athletic directors for 1924–32 period were not available. T.P. Heard (1933–55), Jim Corbett (1956–67), Harry Rabenhorst (1968), Carl Maddox (1969–78), Paul Dietzel (1979–82), Bob Brodhead (1983–86), Joe Dean (1987–).

Tiger — LSU mascot

LOUISIANA TECH UNIVERSITY
Ruston, Louisiana

Joe Aillet Stadium (1968)

Named for Joe Aillet, former Tech coach and athletic director for 26 years. **Lights:** Yes. **Seating capacity:** 30,600. **Location:** On campus. **Playing surface:** Natural grass. **Special features:** Three-level press box seating 67 news media representatives, skybox with theater-type seating for 200, computerized scoreboard with message center in both end zones, bronze Bulldog statue at south end of stadium.

Original construction: 1968, no cost reported. **Additions and renovations:** Addition of skybox to press box in 1985, expansion of seating capacity to current figure in 1989, and installation of new wood-grained lockers for home team in 1997. Cost of these improvements was not reported. They were financed by private donations. **Projected additions:** The construction of Charles Wyly Athletic Center at south end of stadium is planned, but no target date for its completion has been set. The method of financing for this construction has not been determined. **Other uses:** None.

LTU's Bulldog mascot

Team name: Bulldogs. **Team mascot:** Bulldog (live animal). **Colors:** Red and blue. **Song:** Not reported. **Conference:** Independent. **First intercollegiate football game:** 1901.

Coaches and their tenure: Maxie Lambright (1968–78), Larry Beightol and Pat Patterson (1979), Billy Brewer (1980–82), A.L. Williams (1983–86), Carl Torbush (1987), Joe Raymond Peace (1988–95), Gary Crowton (1996–).

Athletic directors and their tenure: Joe Aillet (1968–69), Maxie Lambright (1970–78), Larry Beightol (1979), Charles W. Bussey (1981–83), Bob Vanatta (1984–85), Paul Miller (1986–90), Jerry Stovall (1991–93), Pat Patterson (1994), Jim Oakes (1995–).

UNIVERSITY OF LOUISVILLE
Louisville, Kentucky

Papa John's Cardinal Stadium (1998)

Cardinal of University of Louisville

Lights: Yes. *Seating capacity:* 42,000. *Location:* On campus. *Playing surface:* SportGrass (natural grass grown through a synthetic base). *Special features:* Training and office facility in north end zone, Brown & Williamson club level adjacent to suites and club seating, 29 luxury suites. *Other uses:* None to date.

Original construction: 1998, at a cost of $63 million. Private donations financed the cost of construction. *Projected additions:* None planned.

Team name: Cardinals. *Team mascot:* Cardinal. *Colors:* Red, black, and white. *Song:* "All Hail, U. of L." *Conference:* USA. *First intercollegiate football game:* 1912.

Coaches and their tenure: John L. Smith (1998–).

Athletic directors and their tenure: Tom Jurich (1998–).

MARSHALL UNIVERSITY
Huntington, West Virginia

Marshall University Stadium (1991)

Lights: Yes. *Seating capacity:* 30,000. *Location:* On campus. *Playing surface:* Astroturf. *Special features:* Locker rooms, coaches' offices, 4,332 chair-backed seats, 20 deluxe indoor skyboxes with closed circuit TV and high tech audio systems, scoreboard with video display, and weight/training facility. *Other uses:* Other MU athletic teams may practice on turf due to weather conditions.

Original construction: 1989, at a cost of $30 million. Construction was financed through issuance of bonds and private donations. *Additions and renovations:* Approximately 10,000 seats were added to south end zone in 2000. *Projected additions:* Plans are being made to expand the athletic facilities building in the north end zone, but no target date for this project has been set. Cost of the seat addition in 2000 was $2.5 million, with private donations financing this cost.

Team name: Thundering Herd. *Team mascot:* Marco (costumed figure of buffalo). *Colors:* Kelly green and white. *Song:* "Sons of Marshall." *Conference:* Mid-American. *First intercollegiate football game:* 1898.

Coaches and their tenure: Jim Donnan (1991–95), Bob Pruett (1996–).

Athletic directors and their tenure: Lee Moon (1991–96), Lance West (1997–).

Marco (team mascot)

UNIVERSITY OF MARYLAND
College Park, Maryland

Byrd Stadium (1950)

Named for Dr. H.C. Bryd, former University president and head football coach during period 1911–34.

Lights: Yes. **Seating capacity:** 48,055. **Location:** On campus. **Playing surface:** Natural grass. **Special features:** Five-tier, 90 ft. high press box, 300 luxury suites, and Gossett Football Team House containing locker rooms, weight room, and coaches' offices. **Other uses:** lacrosse games.

Original construction: 1950, cost not reported. **Additions and renovations:** In 1990 the press box was expanded and named Tyser Tower. Four years later an upper deck was added with 12,000 seats. Cost of Gossett Team House was $7 million. Cost of other improvements was not reported, nor was method of financing them.

Team name: Terrapins or Terps. **Team mascot:** Testudo the Terrapin (costumed figure). **Colors:** Red, white, black, and gold. **Song:** "Maryland Victory Song." **Conference:** Atlantic Coast. **First intercollegiate football game:** 1892.

Coaches and their tenure: Jim Tatum (1950–55), Tommy Mont (1956–58), Tom Nugent (1959–65), Lou Saban (1966), Bob Ward (1967–68), Roy Lester (1969–71), Jerry Claiborne (1972–81), Bobby Ross (1982–86), Joe Krivak (1987–91), Mark Duffner (1992–96), Ron Vanderlinden (1997–).

Athletic directors and their tenure: James M. Tatum (1950–55), William W. Cobey (1956–69), James Kehoe (1970–78), Carl James (1979–80), James Kehoe (1981), Richard M. Dull (1982–86), Lew Perkins (1987–90), Andy Geiger (1991–93), Debbie Yow (1994–).

Testudo the Terrapin

UNIVERSITY OF MEMPHIS
Memphis, Tennessee

Liberty Bowl Memorial Stadium (1965)

Named in honor of all veterans of World Wars I and II and the Korean War.

Lights: Yes. **Seating capacity:** 62,380. **Location:** Off campus. **Playing surface:** Prescription turf. **Special features:** Locker rooms, four-level press box with VIP Stadium Club (luxury suites) and elevators. **Other uses:** Liberty Bowl is played here each December, truck and tractor competitions. A Billy Graham Crusade was held here in the 1970s.

Original construction: 1965, at a cost of $3.7 million. **Additions and renovations:** Addition of 12,000 seats, installations of luxury boxes, new lighting system, and new handicapped seating area in 1987. Jumbotron was installed in 1999. Cost of all improvements was $19.5 million. The City of Memphis handled the financing of all construction and renovation costs.

Team name: Tigers. **Team mascot:** Tom II, a live Bengal tiger who is kept at a local zoo and is present at all Tiger home football games and most of their basketball games. **Colors:** Blue and gray. **Song:** "Go Tiger Go." **Conference:** USA. **First intercollegiate football game:** 1912.

Coaches and their tenure: Billy J. Murphy (1965–71), Fred Pancoast (1972–74), Richard Williamson (1975–80), Rex Dockery (1981–83), Rey Dempsey (1984–85), Charlie Bailey (1986–88), Chuck Stobart (1989–94), Rip Scherer (1995–).

Athletic directors and their tenure: Billy J. Murphy (1965–71), Bob Patterson (1981), Charles Cavagnaro (1982–95), R.C. Johnson (1996–).

Tom II

UNIVERSITY OF MIAMI
Coral Gables, Florida

Orange Bowl Stadium (1937)

Lights: Yes. *Seating capacity:* 72,319. *Location:* Off campus. *Playing surface:* Natural grass. *Special features:* Locker rooms. Press box can accommodate 92 journalists plus the scoreboard, public address, and statistics crews as well as live television and radio broadcast crews. *Other uses:* Soccer matches in 1996 Summer Olympic Games were played here. Stadium has been scene of five Super Bowls.

Original construction: 1937, cost not reported. *Additions and renovations:* In 1947 double-decking and construction of wings was completed, together with addition of upper and lower deck seats. East end zone seats were removed in 1977. Expansion of VIP seating and addition of contour seats in 1991 reduced seating capacity. Three years later construction designed to improve handicapped seating further reduced seating capacity. Neither cost nor method of financing these improvements was reported.

Team name: Hurricanes. *Team mascot:* Sebastian the Ibis (costumed figure). *Colors:* Orange, green, and white. *Song:* "Miami U." *Conference:* Big East. *First intercollegiate football game:* 1926.

Coaches and their tenure: Jack Harding (1937–42), Eddie Dunn (1943–44), Jack Harding (1945–47), Andy Gustafson (1948–63), Charlie Tate (1964–69), Walt Kichefski (1970), Fran Curci (1971–72), Pete Elliott (1973–74), Carl Selmer (1975–76), Lou Saban (1977–78), Howard Schnellenberger (1979–83), Jimmy Johnson (1984–88), Dennis Erickson (1989–94), Butch Davis (1995–).

Athletic directors and their tenure: Jack Harding (1948–63), Andy Gustafson (1964–68), Charlie Tate (1969–71), Ernie McCoy (1972–73), Pete Elliott (1974–77), Lou Saban (1978), Dr. Harry Mallios (1979–83), Sam Jankovich (1984–91), Dave Maggard (1992–93), Paul Dee (1994–).

Sebastian the Ibis

MIAMI UNIVERSITY
Oxford, Ohio

Yager Stadium (1983)

Named for Fred C. Yager, a 1914 graduate of Miami University and one of its major benefactors.

Lights: No. **Seating capacity:** 30,012. **Location:** On campus. **Playing surface:** Grass. **Special features:** Locker rooms, training room, classrooms, auxiliary offices for football coaches; offices for soccer coaches; Cradle of Coaches Room used for recruiting, receptions, and meetings. **Other uses:** None.

Original construction: 1983, at a cost of $13.5 million. Private contributions and state funds were used to finance construction. **Additions and renovations:** Seating capacity was increased from 25,000 to current figure in 1996. Cost of this project was $350,000, with private donations financing it.

Team name: Red Hawks. **Team mascot:** "Swoop" (a costumed figure). **Colors:** Red and white. **Song:** "Miami Fight Song." **Conference:** Mid-American. **First intercollegiate football game:** 1888.

Coaches and their tenure: Tim Rose (1983–89), Randy Walker (1990–98), Terry Hoeppner (1999–).

Athletic directors and their tenure: Richard Shrider (1983–89), R.C. Johnson (1990–94), Eric Hyman (1995– 97), Joel Maturi (1998–).

"Swoop"

UNIVERSITY OF MICHIGAN
Ann Arbor, Michigan

Michigan Stadium (1927)

To its many loyal supporters Michigan Stadium is known as "The Big House." It is reportedly the largest University-owned and operated stadium in the United States.

Lights: No. *Seating capacity:* 107,501. *Location:* On campus. *Playing surface:* Natural grass. *Special features:* Locker rooms, press box, new scoreboards and videoboards. *Other uses:* None.

Original construction: 1927, cost not reported. Construction was financed through sale of bonds entitling bond holder to buy season tickets for every season until bonds were retired. *Additions and renovations:* In 1928 1,350 seats were added. Two years later electronic scoreboards were installed at both ends of the stadium. In 1949 seating capacity was increased to 97,239 and wooden bleachers were replaced with steel stands. A state-of-the-art press box, including a photo deck and dark rooms, was built in 1956, the same year that 4,000 seats were added to the stadium. Brick and wrought iron fencing were placed around the stadium concourse in 1997. The following year seats were added around the stadium, with video scoreboards installed in each end zone. Neither the cost nor method of financing these improvements was reported.

Team name: Wolverines. *Team mascot:* Wolverine. *Colors:* Maize and blue. *Song:* "The Victors." *Conference:* Big Ten. *First intercollegiate football game:* 1879.

Coaches and their tenure: Elton E. "Tad" Wieman (1927–28), Harry G. Kipke (1929–37), Herbert O. "Fritz" Crisler (1938–47), Bennie G. Oosterbaan (1948–58), Chalmers W. "Bump" Elliott (1959–68), Glenn E. "Bo" Schembechler (1969–89), Gary O. Moeller (1990–94), Lloyd H. Carr (1995–).

Athletic directors and their tenure: Fielding Yost (1927–41), Fritz Crisler (1942–68), Don Canham (1969–88), Bo Schembechler (1989–90), Jack Weidenbach (1991–94), Joe Roberson (1995–97), Tom A. Goss (1998–).

MICHIGAN STATE UNIVERSITY
East Lansing, Michigan

Spartan Stadium (1923)

Stadium was christened Spartan Stadium in 1957. Prior to that year it was called Macklin Field in honor of former MSU football coach and athletic director John Macklin.

Lights: No. **Seating capacity:** 72,027. **Location:** On campus. **Playing surface:** Artificial turf. **Special features:** Locker rooms, video display board, Stadium Club seats (seven rows of chairback seats between the 20-yard lines on both sides of stadium). **Other uses:** Graduation ceremonies, concerts, movies shown on Diamond Vision screens for students.

Original construction: 1923, no cost reported. **Additions and renovations:** Increased seating capacity to 51,000 in 1948, expanded capacity to 76,000 in 1994 with addition of 9,000 seats, also lowered field eight feet and added Stadium Club seats in 1994. Private donations and Athletic Department funds financed cost of 1994 improvements. Cost of these improvements was not reported.

Team name: Spartans. **Team mascot:** Sparty (costumed figure). **Colors:** Green and white. **Song:** "Spartan Fight Song." **Conference:** Big Ten. **First intercollegiate football game:** 1896.

Coaches and their tenure: Jim Crowley (1923–34), Charles Bachman (1935–46), Clarence "Biggie" Munn (1947–53), Hugh "Duffy" Daugherty (1954–72), Dennis E. Stolz (1973–75), Darryl D. Rogers (1976–79), Frank "Muddy" Watters (1980–82), George J. Perles (1983–94), Nick L. Saban (1995–99), Bobby Williams (2000–).

Athletic directors and their tenure: Ralph H. Young (1923–54), Clarence Munn (1955–72), J. Burt Smith (1973–75), Dr. Joseph Kearney (1976–80), Douglas W. Weaver (1981–90), George Perles (1991–92), Merrily D. Baker (1993–95), Dr. Merritt J. Norvell (1996–98), Clarence Underwood (1999–).

The Spartan

MIDDLE TENNESSEE STATE UNIVERSITY
Murfreesboro, Tennessee

Johnny "Red" Floyd Stadium (1933)

Named for Johnny Floyd, who was head football coach at MTSU in 1917 and during the period 1935–38. He compiled a record of 38 wins and one loss during this period.

Lights: Yes. *Seating capacity:* 30,788. *Location:* On campus. *Playing field surface:* Artificial turf. *Special features:* Five-story press tower seating 60 print news media representatives, camera deck, 16 luxury suites, a weight facility containing more than 10,000 square feet. A Student Athlete Enhancement Center housing individual and group tutor rooms, 80 study carrels, and a computer area opened in 1999. *Other uses:* Local high school football team plays its home games here.

Original construction: 1933; cost not reported. *Additions and renovations:* In 1960 seating capacity was enlarged to 10,000, with 5,000 seats added in 1968. Cost of these additions was not reported. A new press tower, weight room facility, and Student Athlete Enhancement Center were completed in 1999; that same year seating capacity increased from 15,000 to its current figure. Cost of the 1999 improvements was $25 million and was financed by student fees.

Team name: Blue Raiders. *Mascot:* "Lightning," a winged horse. *Colors:* Royal blue and white. *Song:* MTSU Fight Song. *Conference:* Independent at present; will join the Sun Belt in 2001. *First intercollegiate football game:* 1913.

Coaches and their tenure: E.M. Waller (1933–34), Johnny "Red" Floyd (1935–38), Herc Alley (1939), E.W. Midgett (1940–42, 1946), Charles M. Murphy (1947–68), Donald E. Fuoss (1969), Bill Peck (1970–74), Ben Hurt (1975–78), Boots Donnelly (1979–98), Andy McCollum (1999–).

Athletic directors and their tenure: No athletic director was appointed until 1947. Charles Murphy (1947–81), Jimmy Earle (1982–87), John Stanford (1988–93), Lee Fowler (1994–).

Logo for Middle Tennessee State University

University of Minnesota
Minneapolis, Minnesota

Hubert H. Humphrey Metrodome (1982)

Named for Hubert Humphrey, former U.S. senator from Minnesota and Vice-President of the United States. From 1924 to 1981 the Golden Gophers played their home games at Memorial Stadium on campus.

Lights: Yes. *Seating capacity:* 63,669. *Location:* Off campus. *Playing surface:* Astroturf on practice field. *Special features:* Metrodome is the nation's largest air-supported, multiple-use facility. It has 115 luxury boxes, four carpeted locker rooms, and two Jumbotron color replay screens. *Other uses:* Has been site of two World Series, a Super Bowl, an NCAA Final Four, concerts, amateur baseball games, and is the venue for the Minnesota Timberwolves (professional basketball team) home games.

Original construction: 1982, at a cost of $75 million. The sale of revenue bonds, plus interest earned on these bonds, financed construction. *Additions and renovations:* A multi-million dollar plaza recently constructed outside the Metrodome has food and beverages, picnic tables, and a stage for entertainment. The Gibson-Nagurski Football Complex on campus contains a 65,000 square foot indoor practice area and offices for coaches, team meeting room, academic counseling and study rooms, staff conference room, training room, locker rooms, weight room, and players lounge. Cost of the complex was not reported, nor was the method of financing it.

Team name: Golden Gophers. *Team mascot:* "Goldy" Gopher (costumed figure). *Colors:* Maroon and gold. *Song:* "Minnesota Rouser." *Conference:* Big Ten. *First intercollegiate football game:* 1882.

Coaches and their tenure: Joe Salem (1982–83), Lou Holtz (1984–85), John Gutekunst (1986–91), Jim Wacker (1992–96), Glen Mason (1997–).

Athletic directors and their tenure: Paul Giel (1982–87), Rick Bay (1988–91), Dr. McKinley Boston (1992–95), Dr. Mark Dienhart (1996–).

UNIVERSITY OF MISSISSIPPI
Oxford, Mississippi

Vaught-Hemingway Stadium (1915)

Named for John Vaught, head football coach at Ole Miss for 25 years, and Judge William Hemingway, Ole Miss law professor and long-time chairman of the University Athletics Committee.

Lights: Yes. **Seating capacity:** 50,577. **Location:** On campus. **Playing surface:** Grass. **Special features:** Luxury suites on west side and 1,000-seat luxury suites on east side. **Other uses:** None.

Original construction: 1915, cost not reported. **Additions:** Seating capacity was increased in 1988 and again in 1998. Cost of 1988 expansion was $5 million, with the 1998 expansion costing $10.7 million. Private donations, Loyalty Foundation gifts, and issuance of bonds financed both these enlargements.

Team name: Rebels. **Team mascot:** Colonel Rebel. **Colors:** Cardinal red and navy blue. **Song:** "Forward Rebels." **Conference:** Southeastern. **First intercollegiate football game:** 1893.

Coaches and their tenure: Fred Robbins (1915–16), C.R.(Dudy) Noble (1917–18), R.L. Sullivan (1919–21), R.A. Cowell (1922–23), Chester Barnard (1924), Homer Hazel (1925–29), Ed L. Walker (1930–37), Harry J. Mehre (1938–45), Harold (Red) Drew (1946), John H. Vaught (1947–70), Billy R. Kinard (1971–73), Ken Cooper (1974–77), Steve Sloan (1978–82), Billy Brewer (1983–93), Joe Lee Dunn (1994), Tommy Tuberville (1995–98), David Cutcliffe (1999–).

Athletic directors and their tenure: Tad Smith (1946–71), Bruiser Kinard (1972), John Vaught (1973–78), Warner Alford (1979–94), Pete Boone (1995–98), John Shafer (1999–).

Colonel Rebel

MISSISSIPPI STATE UNIVERSITY
Mississippi State, Mississippi

Scott Field (1914)

Named for Don Magruder Scott, football star and Olympic sprinter at MSU.

Lights: Yes. *Seating capacity:* 40,656. *Location:* On campus. *Playing surface:* Prescription athletic turf. *Special features:* Locker rooms, press box, Jumbotron. *Other uses:* Commencement exercises (President George Bush gave the commencement address here in 1990).

Original construction: 1914, cost not reported. *Additions and renovations:* Seating capacity was expanded in 1936 and again in 1948, when 9,000 seats were added, bringing capacity to its current figure. Extensive renovations were completed in 1985-86. Five years later locker rooms were refurbished and a Center was built for the Seal M-Club, a University athletic booster group. Cost of the 1985-86 renovations was $7.2 million, with the 1991 improvements costing $1.4 million. A bond issue, private donations, and the sale of luxury boxes financed both improvements. *Projected additions:* Expansion of the seating capacity to 52,000, addition of chairbacks and luxury boxes on the east side, renovation of locker rooms, and building of a media services room will be completed by 2001. The estimated cost for this project has not been reported. Part of its financing will come from the sale of luxury boxes.

Team name: Bulldogs. *Team mascot:* Bully (a live dog). *Colors:* Maroon and white. *Song:* "Hail State." *Conference:* Southeastern. *First intercollegiate football game:* 1895.

Coaches and their tenure: E.C. Hayes (1914–16), Sid Robinson (1917–19), Fred Holtkamp (1920–21), C.R. "Dudy" Noble (1922), Earl Able (1923–24), Bernie Bierman (1925–26), J.W. Hancock (1927–29), Chris Cagle (1930), Ray Dauber (1931–32), Ross McKechnie (1933–34), Ralph Sasse (1935–37), Spike Nelson (1938), Allyn McKeen (1939–48), Slick Morton (1949–51), Murray Warmath (1952–53), Darrell Royal (1954–55), Wade Walker (1956–61), Paul Davis (1962–66), Charley Sharp (1967–72), Bob Tyler (1973–78), Emory Ballard (1979–85), Rockey Felker (1986–90), Jackie Sherrill (1991–).

Athletic directors and their tenure: William Dale Chadwick (1914–30), C.R. Noble (1931–34), Ralph I. Sasse (1935–36), Paul B. Parker (1937), C.R. Noble (1938–59), Wade Walker (1960–66), Charley Saira (1972–76), Bob Tyler (1977–79), Carl Maddox (1980–83), Dr. Charley Scott (1984–86), Charley Carr (1987), Larry Templeton (1988–).

Opposite, inset: Bully (mascot for MSU)

UNIVERSITY OF MISSOURI
Columbia, Missouri

Memorial Stadium/Faurot Field (1926)

Named for Don Faurot, former football coach and athletic director at the University who served in these two positions for 32 years.

Lights: Yes. **Seating capacity:** 62,000. **Location:** On campus. **Playing surface:** Grass. **Special features:** Diamond Vision scoreboard, home dressing room which includes a sports medicine center with X-ray lab, a 100-seat interview room, and a legends wall. **Other uses:** Concerts, community events.

Original construction: 1926, at a cost of $350,000. **Additions and renovations:** Several expansions of the seating capacity were made during the period 1948–78. In 1997 extensive renovations were made to the concourses, restrooms, concession stands, parking lots, and a new north entry plaza was built with team store, box office, etc. Cost of these improvements was $12 million, which was financed from the sale of revenue bonds, a ticket surcharge, and revenue from the sale of suite premium seats. **Projected additions:** A new press box with 32 luxury suites is planned for use during the 2000 season. Estimated cost of this project is $10.2 million.

Team name: Tigers. **Team mascot:** Truman the Tiger (costumed figure). **Colors:** Old gold and black. **Song:** "Every True Son." **Conference:** Big 12. **First intercollegiate football game:** 1890.

Coaches and their tenure: Gwinn Henry (1926–31), Frank Carideo (1932–34), Don Faurot (1935–42), Chauncey Simpson (1943–45), Don Faurot (1946–56), Frank Broyles (1957), Dan Devine (1958–70), Al Onofrio (1971–77), Warren Powers (1978–84), Woody Widenhofer (1985–88), Bob Stull (1989–93), Larry Smith (1994–).

Athletic directors and their tenure: Chester L. Brewer (1926–34), Don Faurot (1935–42), George Edwards (1943–45), Don Faurot (1946–66), Dan Devine (1967–70), Wilbur Stalcup (1971–72), Mel Sheehan (1972–77), Dave Hart (1978–86), Jack Lengyel (1987–88), Dick Tomburo (1989–92), Dan Devine (1993–94), Joe Castiglione (1995–97), Michael Alden (1998–).

Truman the Tiger

UNIVERSITY OF NEBRASKA
Lincoln, Nebraska

Memorial Stadium (1923)

Named to honor all Nebraskans who served in the Civil and Spanish-American Wars, the 751 Nebraskans who died in World War I, the 3,839 in World War II, the 225 in Korea, and the 422 in Vietnam.

Lights: Yes. *Seating capacity:* 72,200. *Location:* On campus. *Playing surface:* Artificial turf. *Special features:* Locker rooms, medical facilities, strength complex, post-game interview room, offices for coaches and athletic administrators, N Club Lounge, and performance buffet. *Other uses:* Site for team practice sessions.

Original construction: 1923, at cost of $430,000. *Additions and renovations:* South end zone section was built in 1964, making the stadium a horseshoe and raising seating capacity to 48,000. In 1965 this figure was increased to 53,000. The following year 12,000 seats were added and stadium was converted into a bowl. In 1972 the south end zone was extended and 9,400 seats were added. Hewit Center, a dining area/study hall, was completed in West Stadium. Section 14 of stadium was remodeled to accommodate disabled in 1994. Cost of these improvements was not reported. During period 1997–99 a new press box was installed, concourses were renovated, stadium view lounge was constructed. In addition, a club seating area and 42 skyboxes were added. Cost of these improvements was $36 million, all financed by private donations.

Team name: Huskers. *Team mascot:* Herbie Husker and "Lil Red." *Colors:* Scarlet and cream. *Song:* "No Place Like Nebraska." *Conference:* Big 12. *First intercollegiate football game:* 1891.

Coaches and their tenure: Fred Dawson (1923–24), Ernest E. Bearg (1925–28), Dana X. Bible (1929–36), Lawrence "Biff" Jones (1937–41), Glenn Presnell (1942), Adolph J. Lewandowski (1943–44), George "Potsy" Clark (1945–48), Bernie Masterson (1946–47), Bill Glassford (1949–55), Pete Elliott (1956), Bill Jennings (1957–61), Bob Devaney (1962–72), Tom Osborne (1973–97), Frank Solich (1998–).

Athletic directors and their tenure: H.D. Gish (1928–31), Dana X. Bible (1932–36), Lawrence "Biff" Jones (1937–42), A.J. Lewandowski (1943–47), George "Potsy" Clark (1948–53), J.W. Bill Orwig (1954–60), Charles Miller and Joseph Soshink (1961), Tippy Dye (1962–66), Bob Devaney (1967–93), Bill Byrne (1994–).

Opposite, inset: Logo for Nebraska Huskers

UNIVERSITY OF NEVADA–LAS VEGAS
Las Vegas, Nevada

Sam Boyd Stadium (1971)

Sam Boyd was a gaming and hotel mogul who gave $1 million to buy artificial turf for the playing field in 1984.

Lights: Yes. **Seating capacity:** 40,000. **Location:** Off campus (in desert). **Playing surface:** Grass. **Special features:** Horseshoe shape is being retained so picturesque mountain view may be enjoyed by spectators. **Other uses:** Concerts and festivals, motorcross and state high school games and championship. Three WAC championship games have been played here, and stadium is site of the annual Las Vegas Bowl.

Original construction: 1971, at a cost of $3.5 million. **Additions and renovations:** In 1999 8,000 seats were added to bring capacity to current figure. A state-of-the-art press box tower was built which includes 12 luxury boxes. A new concourse and façade was constructed, and grass replaced the artificial turf. Cost of these improvements was $18 million. State funds, Las Vegas Convention & Visitors Bureau funds, and private donations financed this cost.

Team name: Rebels. **Team mascot:** Hey Reb. **Colors:** Scarlet and gray. **Song:** "Win with the Rebels." **Conference:** Mountain West. **First intercollegiate football game:** 1968.

Coaches and their tenure: Bill Ireland (1968–72), Ron Meyer (1973–75), Tony Knap (1976–81), Harvey Hyde (1982–85), Wayne Nunnely (1986–89), Jim Strong (1990–93), Jeff Horton (1994–98), John Robinson (1999–).

Athletic directors and their tenure: Chub Drakulich (1968–72), Bill Ireland (1973–79), Al Negratti (1980), Brad Rothermel (1981–90), Jim Weaver, (1991–94), Charles Cavagnaro (1995–).

Hey Reb

UNIVERSITY OF NEVADA–RENO
Reno, Nevada

Mackay Stadium (1966)

Named in memory of John Mackay, a Comstock mining millionaire during the 19th century. His son Clarence donated the necessary money to construct a stadium.

Lights: No. *Seating capacity:* 31,545. *Location:* On campus. *Playing surface:* Natural grass. *Special features:* 60 luxury suites. Cashell Fieldhouse houses coaches' offices, weight room, orthopedic clinic, and film rooms. *Other uses:* None.

Original construction: 1966, at a cost of $800,000. State funds and private donations financed the cost of construction. *Additions and renovations:* Seats were added in each of the following years: 1977, 1979, 1985, 1989, and 1992. Thirty sky boxes were built in 1981, and in 1995 30 additional sky boxes were constructed. The first scoreboard was installed in 1983; a new scoreboard was installed in 1995. Total cost of these improvements was $15 million, with financing made possible by private donations and state funds.

Team name: Wolf Pack. *Team mascot:* Arctic wolf (costumed figure). *Colors:* Navy blue and silver. *Song:* "Hail, Sturdy Men." *Conference:* Western Athletic. *First intercollegiate football game:* 1898.

Coaches and their tenure: Dick Trachok (1966–68), Jerry Scattini (1969–75), Chris Ault (1976–92), Jeff Horton (1993), Chris Ault (1994–95), Jeff Tisdel (1996–).

Athletic directors and their tenure: Jake Lawlor (1966–68), Dick Trachok (1969–86), Chris Ault (1987–).

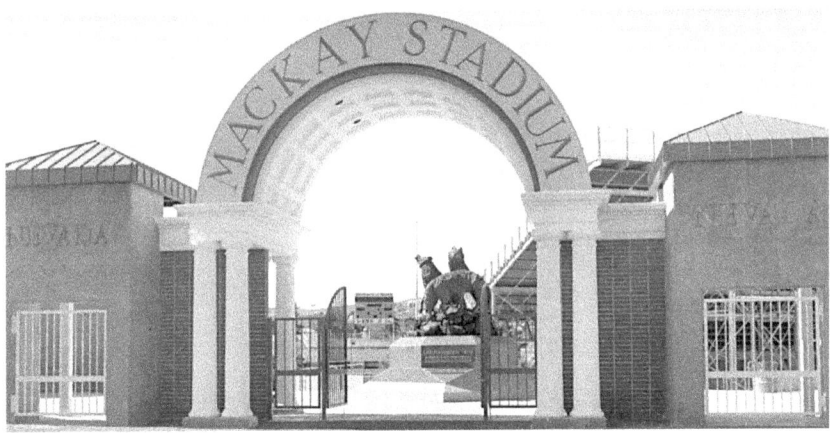

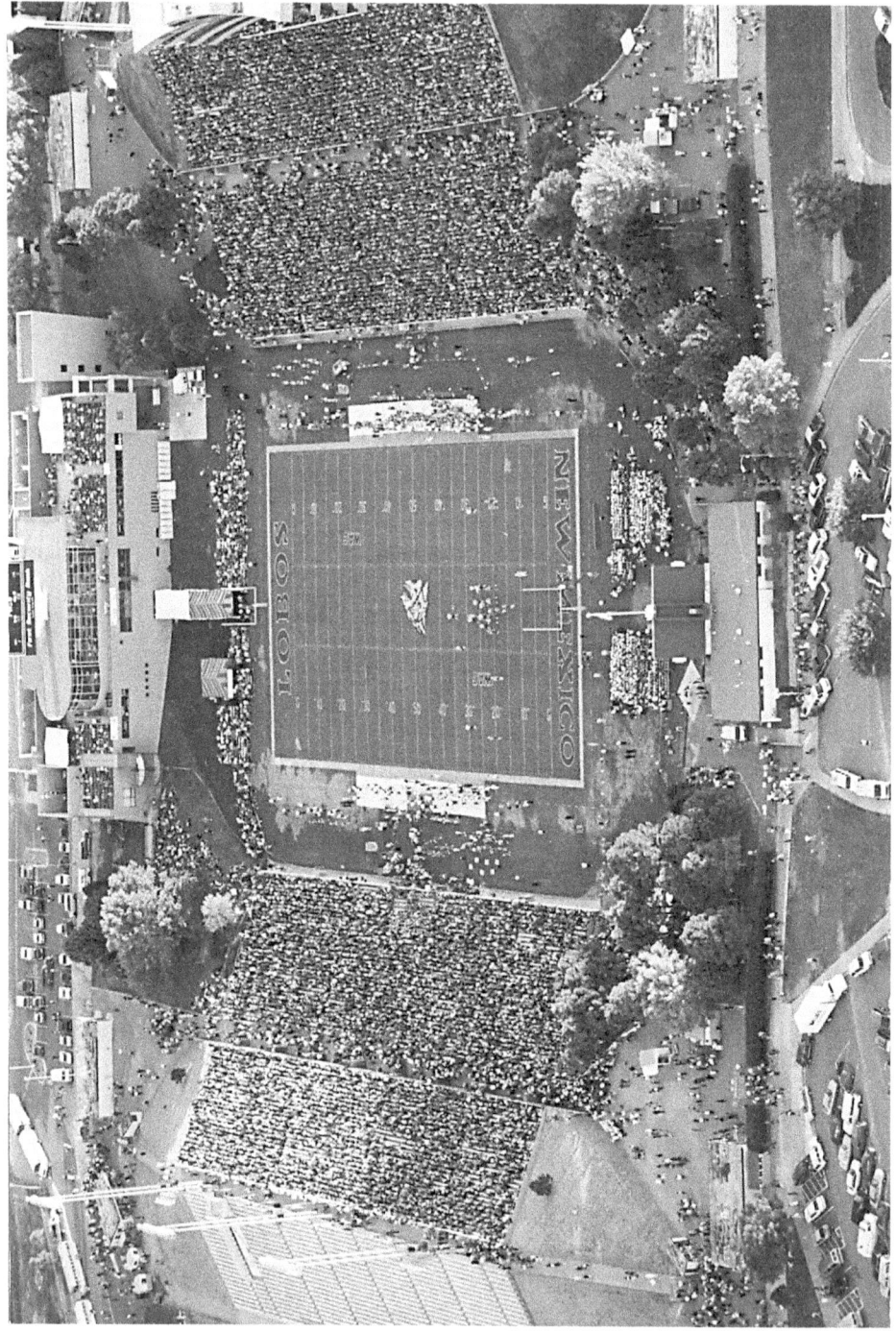

UNIVERSITY OF NEW MEXICO
Albuquerque, New Mexico

University Stadium (1960)

Lights: Yes. *Seating capacity:* 31,218. *Location:* On campus. *Playing surface:* Grass. *Special features:* L.F. "Tow" Diehm Facility in south end zone includes weight room, locker room, equipment room, coaches' offices, meeting rooms, and sports medicine center. *Other uses:* Commencement exercises, occasional concerts.

Original construction: 1960, at a cost of $750,000. *Additions and renovations:* In 1976 a press box with a seating capacity of 646, including luxury suites, was added. A training facility and office/meeting complex was renovated in 1995. The 1976 project cost was $1.8 million, with $8 million as the cost for the 1995 renovation. Revenue from the sale of University property and general University funds financed the cost of these improvements. *Projected additions:* Additional seating in the sound end zone is planned, but no target date has been set for this project, which is estimated to cost $18 million.

Team name: Lobos. *Team mascot:* Lobo Louie (costumed figure). *Colors:* Cherry and silver. *Song:* "The UNM Fight Song." *Conference:* Mountain West. *First intercollegiate football game:* 1894.

Coaches and their tenure: Bill Weeks (1960–67), Rudy Feldman (1968–73), Bill Mondt (1974–79), Joe Morrison (1980–82), Joe Lee Dunn (1983–86), Mike Sheppard (1987–91), Dennis Franchione (1992–97), Rocky Long (1998–).

Athletic directors and their tenure: Pete McDavid (1960–74), Lavon McDonald (1975–78), John Bridgers (1979–86), John Koenig (1987–88), Gary Ness (1989–92), Rudy Davalos (1993–).

Lobo Louie (mascot for University of New Mexico)

NEW MEXICO STATE UNIVERSITY
Las Cruces, New Mexico

Aggie Memorial Stadium (1977)

Named in memory of Korean and Vietnam War veterans associated with the University.

Lights: Yes. *Seating capacity:* 33,000. *Location:* On campus. *Playing surface:* Grass. *Special features:* Locker rooms, press box seating approximately 100 news media personnel. *Other uses:* None.

Original construction: 1977, at a cost of $4 million. Construction was financed by a capital expenditure fund. *Additions and renovations:* None to date, none projected.

Team name: Aggies. *Team mascot:* Pistol Pete (costumed figure wearing a cowboy outfit). *Colors:* Crimson and white. *Song:* "Aggie Fight Song." *Conference:* Big West. *First intercollegiate football game:* 1894.

Coaches and their tenure: Jim Bradley (1977), Gil Krueger (1978–82), Fred Zechman (1983–85), Mike Knoll (1986–89), Jim Hess (1990–96), Tony Samuel (1977–).

Athletic directors and their tenure: Keith Colson (1977–86), Al Gonzales (1987–96), Jim Paul (1997–98), Brian Faison (1999–).

Pistol Pete

UNIVERSITY OF NORTH CAROLINA
Chapel Hill, North Carolina

Kenan Memorial Stadium (1927)

Named for William Rand Kenan, Jr., UNC alumnus and international industrialist who made substantial contributions to the University.

Lights: Yes. *Seating capacity:* 60,000. *Location:* On campus. *Playing surface:* Grass. *Special features:* Kenan Football Center, a four-level structure housing coaches' offices, locker rooms, weight room, training room, computer labs and study areas, 100+ seat auditorium, theater, and Hall of Honor. *Other uses:* Commencement exercises, state high school championship football games.

Original construction: 1926, at a cost of $303,000. *Additions and renovations:* Seating capacity has been expanded several times, the latest in 1997–98. Each time great care has been taken to preserve its beauty. In 1977 Kenan Fieldhouse was enlarged to 30,000 square feet. In 1986 the Student Athlete Development Center was added to the Fieldhouse. Eight thousand seats were added in 1997–98. At the same time the Kenan Football Center was constructed. Cost of this addition and construction was $45 million, which was financed by the sale of revenue-generating bonds and private donations.

Team name: Tar Heels. *Team mascot:* Rameses 29, a live ram. *Colors:* Carolina blue and white. *Song:* "Here Comes Carolina." *Conference:* Atlantic Coast. *First intercollegiate football game:* 1894.

Coaches and their tenure: Chuck Collins (1927–33), Carl Snavely (1934–35), Ray Wolf (1936–41), Jim Tatum (1942), Tom Young (1943), Gene McEver (1944), Carl Snavely (1945–52), George Barclay (1953–55), Jim Tatum (1956–58), Jim Hickey (1959–66), Bill Dooley (1967–77), Dick Crum (1978–87), Mack Brown (1988–97), Carl Torbush (1998–).

Athletic directors and their tenure: Robert Fetzer (1927–52), Charles P. "Chuck" Erickson (1953–68), Homer Rice (1969–75), William Cobey (1976–79), John Swofford (1980–96), Richard A. Baddour (1997–).

Logo for UNC Tar Heels

NORTH CAROLINA STATE UNIVERSITY
Raleigh, North Carolina

Carter-Finley Stadium (1966)

Named after Harry and Nick Carter, NCSU alumni and textile executives, and the late Raleigh philanthropist A.E. Finley.

Lights: Yes. **Seating capacity:** 51,500. **Location:** Off campus. **Playing surface:** Grass. **Special features:** Press box seating 213, two-level A.E. Finley Fieldhouse with team dressing rooms on lower level and reception area on upper level. **Other uses:** Concerts, commencement exercises, site for some events in the World Special Olympic Games in the summer of 1999.

Original construction: 1964, at a cost of $3.7 million. The North Carolina Department of Agriculture donated the land for the stadium. **Additions and renovations:** None. **Projected additions:** Construction of a state-of-the-art facility in the south end zone is planned for the early years of the 21st century. This facility will house locker rooms, weight and training rooms, players' lounge, an area for recruits, football offices, and a Hall of Fame for all sports. In addition, a new press box, luxury suites, ticket office, and new offices for the Wolfpack Club are planned. Estimated cost of these facilities is $50 million. The method of financing this construction was not reported.

Team name: Wolfpack. **Team mascot:** Mr. and Mrs. Wuf (costumed figures). **Colors:** Red and white. **Song:** "State College Keeps Fighting Along." **Conference:** Atlantic Coast. **First intercollegiate football game:** 1893.

Coaches and their tenure: Earle Edwards (1966–70), Al Michaels (1971), Lou Holtz (1972–75), Bo Rein (1976–79), Monte Kiffin (1980–82), Tom Reed (1983–85), Dick Sheridan (1986–92), Mike O'Cain (1993–99), Chuck Amato (2000–).

Athletic directors and their tenure: Roy B. Clogston (1966–68), Willis Casey (1969–85), Jim Valvano (1986–89), Todd Turner (1990–95), Les Robinson (1996–).

Mr. and Mrs. Wuf

UNIVERSITY OF NORTH TEXAS
Denton, Texas

Fouts Field (1951)

Named for Thereon J. Fouts, former athletic director and head football and basketball coach for 15 years who was instrumental in stadium construction.

Lights: Yes. **Seating capacity:** 30,500. **Location:** On campus. **Playing surface:** Artificial turf. **Special features:** Locker rooms, two banquet rooms seating 200.

Original construction: 1950, cost not reported. **Additions:** In 1994 10,000 seats were added in the two end zones at a cost of $1 million. An increase in student services fees financed the cost of this addition. **Other uses:** Concerts, track meets, charity events.

Team name: Eagles, Mean Green. **Team mascot:** Scrappy. **Colors:** Green and white. **Song:** "UNT Fight Song." **Conference:** Big West. **First intercollegiate football game:** 1913.

Coaches and their tenure: Odus Mitchell (1951–66), Rod Rust (1967–72), Hayden Fry (1973–78), Jerry Moore (1979–80), Bob Tyler (1981), Corky Nelson (1982–90), Dennis Parker (1991–93), Matt Simon (1994–97), Darrell Dickey (1998–).

Athletic directors and their tenure: Thereon J. Fouts (1951–54), Emmett F. Cambron (1954–60), Jess E. Cearley (1961–67), Rod Rust (1968–71), Fred McCain (1972), Hayden Fry (1973–78), Andy Everest (1979–80), Bob Tyler (1981–82), Fred McCain (1983–87), Richard McDuffie (1988–89), Corky Nelson (1990–91), Steve Sloan (1992–93), Craig Helwig (1994–).

Scrappy

NORTHEAST LOUISIANA UNIVERSITY
Monroe, Louisiana

Malone Stadium (1978)

Formerly known as Indian Stadium, Malone Stadium is named for James L. Malone, head football coach at NLU during the period 1934–53.

Lights: Yes. **Seating capacity:** 30,427. **Location:** On campus. **Playing surface:** Grass. **Special features:** Locker rooms, luxury boxes, tutor rooms, video sports lab, computer lab, equipment room, sports medicine complex, and offices for coaches and athletic administrators. **Other uses:** None.

Original construction: 1978, at cost of $6,579,400, including land acquisition, stadium, and fieldhouse. **Additions and renovations:** In 1983 seating capacity was increased by 3,277, with east side stands extended into each end zone. In 1985 Booster Skybox was renovated and expanded. The press box was enlarged with the addition of two camera decks in 1991. Two years later 8,350 seats were added, bringing seating capacity to current figure. Neither the cost of these improvements nor the method of financing them was reported.

Team name: Indians. **Team mascot:** Chief Brave Spirit. **Colors:** Maroon and gold. **Song:** "NLU Fight Song." **Conference:** Independent. **First intercollegiate football game:** 1931 as a junior college, 1951 as a senior college.

Coaches and their tenure: John David Crow (1978–80), Pat Collins (1981–88), Dave Roberts (1989–93), Ed Zaunbrecher (1994–98), Bobby Keasler (1999–).

Athletic directors and their tenure: Benny Hollis (1980–94), Richard Giannini (1995–).

Chief Brave Spirit

NORTHERN ILLINOIS UNIVERSITY
DeKalb, Illinois

Huskie Stadium (1965)

Lights: Yes. *Seating capacity:* 31,000. *Location:* On campus. *Playing surface:* Astroturf. *Special features:* Locker rooms, classrooms, coaches' offices, sky box, auxiliary TV press box, Speed & Strength Complex, Hall of Fame. *Other uses:* Teams representing eight other intercollegiate sports play here, Drum Corps Midwest championship held here annually.

Original construction: 1965, at a cost of $2,265,172. *Additions and renovations:* In 1982 seating capacity was expanded by 5,750 seats. New lights were erected, public address system was revamped, and two meeting rooms were built in 1993. Two years later a new, modern steel and aluminum east grandstand that matches the curve and design of the original stadium (west side) was added. *Projected additions:* Construction of a sports medicine and equipment center, installation of additional locker facilities, and renovation of existing skybox and press box has been discussed. No target date or cost estimate for this project has been reported. Revenue from issuance of bonds and private donations financed cost of 1995 improvements, which was $4 million.

Team name: Huskies. *Team mascot:* Victor E. Huskie. *Colors:* Cardinal and black. *Song:* "Huskie Fight Song." *Conference:* Mid-American. *First intercollegiate football game:* 1901.

Coaches and their tenure: Howard Fletcher (1965–68), Richard Urich (1969–70), Jerry Ippoliti (1971–75), Pat Culpepper (1976–79), Bill Mallory (1980–83), Leo Corso (1984), Jerry Pettibone (1985–90), Charlie Sadler (1991–95), Joe Novak (1996–).

Athletic directors and their tenure: George "Chick" Evans (1965–68), Bob Brigham (1969–86), Jim Mellard (1987), Gerald O'Dell (1988–94), Cary Groth (1995–).

Victor E. Huskie logo

NORTHWESTERN UNIVERSITY
Evanston, Illinois

Ryan Field (1942)

Named for family of Patrick G. Ryan, who has been a member of the University Board of Trustees since 1978. His wife Shirley Ryan has been a member of Northwestern's Women's Board since that same year.

Lights: Yes. **Seating capacity:** 47,130. **Location:** On campus. **Playing surface:** Natural grass. **Special features:** Locker rooms, equipment room, sports medicine center, team meeting area, three-tier press box with enclosed Stadium Club seating 300, seating for disabled spectators on both sides of stadium. **Other uses:** None.

Original construction: 1942, at a cost of $1,425,000. **Additions and renovations:** In 1949 stadium was enlarged by the construction of a horseshoe enclosure at sound end. Improvements in 1996–97 included additional seating to bring capacity to current figure, press box renovation, building a multi-purpose indoor practice facility, and replacement of artificial turf with natural grass. Cost of these improvements was $20 million, financed by a fund-raising campaign for athletic facilities.

Team name: Wildcats. **Team mascot:** Willie the Wildcat (costumed figure). **Colors:** Purple and white. **Song:** "Go! U Northwestern." **Conference:** Big Ten. **First intercollegiate football game:** 1882.

Coaches and their tenure: Lynn Waldorf (1942–46), Bob Voigts (1947–54), Lou Saban (1955), Ara Parseghian (1956–63), Alex Agase (1964–72), John Pont (1973–77), Rick Ventura (1978–80), Dennis Green (1981–85), Francis Peay (1986–91), Gary Barnett (1992–98), Randy Walker 1999–).

Athletic directors and their tenure: Kenneth L. Wilson (1942–44), Thodore B. Payseur (1945–55), Stuart K. Holcomb (1956–66), W.H.H. "Tippy" Dye (1967–74), John Pont (1975–80), Doug Single (1981–86), Bruce Corrie (1987–92), Bill Foster (1993), Rick Taylor (1994–).

Northwestern University wildcat logo

UNIVERSITY OF NOTRE DAME
Notre Dame, Indiana

Notre Dame Stadium (1930)

Lights: Yes. *Seating capacity:* 80,012. *Location:* On campus. *Playing surface:* Natural grass. *Special features:* Expanded locker rooms for both Notre Dame and visiting team, three-tier press box with seating for 300 media personnel in main part, which contains three television and five radio broadcast booths. *Other uses:* Pep rallies.

Original construction: 1930, at a cost of more than $750,000. *Additions and renovations:* 21,000 seats were added during the period 1995–97. During the same period a three-tier press box was built, locker rooms were enlarged, two new dot-matrix message center scoreboards were installed, and restrooms and concession stands were expanded. These improvements, costing $50 million, were financed by tax-exempt, fixed-rate bonds.

Team name: Fighting Irish. *Team mascot:* Leprechaun (costumed figure). *Colors:* Gold and blue. *Song:* "Notre Dame Victory March." *Conference:* Independent. *First intercollegiate football game:* 1887.

Coaches and their tenure: Knute Rockne (1930), Heartley "Hunk" Anderson (1931–33), Elmer Layden (1934–40), Frank Leahy (1941–43), Ed McKeever (1944), Hugh Devore (1945), Frank Leahy (1946–53), Terry Brennan (1954–58), Joe Kuharich (1959–62), Hugh Devore (1963), Ara Parseghian (1964–74), Dan Devine (1975–80), Gerry Faust (1981–85), Lou Holtz (1986–96), Bob Davie (1997–).

Athletic directors and their tenure: Knute Rockne (1930), Jesse Harper (1931–33), Elmer Layden (1934–40), Hugh Devore (1945), Frank Leahy (1947–48), Edward "Moose" Krause (1949–81), Gene Corrigan (1982–87), Dick Rosenthal (1987–95), Mike Wadsworth (1996–).

Leprechaun logo for University of Notre Dame

OHIO STATE UNIVERSITY
Columbus, Ohio

Ohio Stadium (1922)

Lights: Yes. *Seating capacity:* 89,841. *Location:* On campus. *Playing surface:* Prescription athletic turf (grass). *Special features:* State-of-the-art scoreboard, press box. *Other uses:* Occasional concerts, site of home games for the Columbus Crew, a professional soccer team.

Original construction: 1922, at a cost of $1,341,000. *Additions and renovations:* In 1991 5,000 seats were added to bring the capacity to its current figure. *Projected additions:* An extensive renovation program is planned. This includes the erection of 82 private suites and 2,500 club seats, wider aisles, expanded concession stands, improved seating for the disabled, modernized restrooms, additional elevators and escalators, and the addition of 8,000 seats. Target date for completion of this program is 2001. Estimated cost of these improvements is $150 million, with the cost to be financed by revenue from an extra fee in the price of game tickets, revenue from the sale of suites and club seats, and private donations.

Team name: Buckeyes. *Team mascot:* Brutus Buckeye (costumed figure). *Colors:* Scarlet and gray. *Song:* "Buckeye Battle Cry." *Conference:* Big Ten. *First intercollegiate football game:* 1890.

Coaches and their tenure: John W. Wilce (1922–28), Sam S. Willaman (1929–33), Francis A. Schmidt (1934–40), Paul E. Brown (1941–43), Carroll C. Widdoes (1944–45), Paul O. Bixler (1946), Wesley E. Fesler (1947–50), W.W. "Woody" Hayes (1951–78), Earle Bruce (1979–87), John Cooper (1988–).

Athletic directors and their tenure: Lynn St. John (1922–47), Dick Larkins (1948–70), Ed Weaver (1971–77), Hugh Hindman (1978–84), Rick Bay (1985–87), Jim Jones (1988–93), Andy Geiger (1994–).

Logo for Ohio State University

OHIO UNIVERSITY
Athens, Ohio

Peden Stadium (1929)

Named for Don Peden, head football coach at Ohio University for 17 years.

Lights: Yes. *Seating capacity:* 20,000. *Location:* On campus. *Playing surface:* Grass. *Special features:* Press box, scoreboard, locker room, coaches' offices, sky boxes for Stadium Tower Club, an athletic program support group. *Other uses:* Track surrounding stadium is used for track and field meets, including the annual Ohio Invitational.

Original construction: 1929, cost not reported. *Additions and renovations:* In 1985 seating capacity was increased to its current figure. That same year a five-level tower was constructed as the stadium front. This facility houses coaches' offices, locker rooms, equipment room, classrooms, and a weight training facility. No data on the cost or method of financing these improvements was reported.

Team name: Bobcats. *Team mascot:* Bobcat (costumed figure). *Colors:* Hunter green and white. *Song:* "Stand Up and Cheer." *Conference:* Mid-American. *First intercollegiate football game:* 1894.

Coaches and their tenure: Don Peden (1929–46), Harold Wise (1947–48), Carroll Widdoes (1949–57), Bill Hess (1958–77), Bob Kappes (1978), Brian Burke (1979–84), Cleve Bryant (1985–89), Tom Lichtenberg (1990–94), Jim Grobe (1995–).

Athletic directors and their tenure: Ossian Clinton Bird (1929–37), Don Peden (1938–47), Harold Wise (1948), Carroll Widdoes (1949–61), Brandon T. "Butch" Grover (1962–63), William D. Rohr (1964–67), Harold McElhaney (1978– 95), Thomas C. Boeh (1996–)

Ohio University Bobcats logo

UNIVERSITY OF OKLAHOMA
Norman, Oklahoma

Oklahoma Memorial Stadium (1925)

Named in memory of University alumni and other associated persons who died in World War I.

Lights: Yes. *Seating capacity:* 75,004. *Location:* On campus. *Playing surface:* Grass. *Special features:* Locker rooms, 12 sky suites. *Other uses:* None.

Original construction: 1925, at a cost of $293,000. *Additions and renovations:* With the completion of the south end zone in 1980, seating capacity was increased. The Barry Switzer Center, named in honor of a former coach, was completed in 1999 and houses the weight room, training room, equipment room, meeting rooms, Hall of Fame, coaches offices, and a large auditorium. Cost of this center was $5.7 million, which was financed by the issuance of bonds and private donations.

Team name: Sooners. *Team mascot:* Sooner Schooner (a covered wagon). *Colors:* Crimson and cream. *Song:* "Boomer Schooner." *Conference:* Big 12. *First intercollegiate football game:* 1895.

Coaches and their tenure: Bennie Owen (1925–26), Adrian Lindsey (1927–31), Lewie Hardage (1932–34), Lawrence "Biff" Jones (1935–36), Tom Stidham (1937–40), Dewey "Snorter" Luster (1941–45), Jim Tatum (1946), Bud Wilkinson (1947–63), Gomer Jones (1964–65), Jim MacKenzie (1966), Chuck Fairbanks (1967–72), Barry Switzer (1973–88), Gary Gibbs (1989–94), Howard Schnellenberger (1995), John Blake (1996–98), Bob Stoops (1999–).

Athletic directors and their tenure: Ben G. Owen (1925–35), Lawrence Jones (1936), Tom Stidham (1937–41), Lawrence Haskell (1942), Dale Arbuckle (1943–46), Lawrence Haskell (1947), Charles "Bud" Wilkinson (1948–64), Gomer Jones (1965–72), Wade Walker (1973–88), Donnie Duncan (1989–95), Steve Owens (1996), Joe Castiglione (1997–).

Sooner Schooner

OKLAHOMA STATE UNIVERSITY
Stillwater, Oklahoma

Lewis Field (1920)

Named for Dr. Laymon Lowery Lewis, former dean of veterinary medicine at OSU and one of the most popular figures in the University's history. He was instrumental in the development of experimental stations throughout Oklahoma.

Lights: Yes. **Seating capacity:** 50,614. **Location:** On campus. **Playing surface:** Artificial turf. **Special features:** Locker rooms, press box with VIP seating for 300. **Other uses:** Commencement exercises, Special Olympics site, Orange Peel.

Original construction: 1920, cost not reported. **Additions and renovations:** Additional seats were erected in 1924 and again in 1929. In 1947 seating capacity was expanded to 30,000. Three years later 10,000 seats were added on the north side. The field was lowered and seating added on both sides in 1971. In 1978 a Coaches Building was constructed with offices for coaches and the athletic director as well as a Varsity Club lounge. A press box was erected in 1980 at a cost of $2.5 million. Lights were installed in 1985 at a cost of $750,000. In 1987 Astroturf was installed at a cost of $400,000. Private donations provided the funds for all these improvements.

Team name: Cowboys. **Team mascot:** Pistol Pete (costumed figure wearing a cowboy outfit). **Colors:** Orange and black. **Song:** "Ride Cowboy Ride." **Conference:** Big 12. **First intercollegiate football game:** 1901.

Coaches and their tenure: James E. Pixlee (1920), John F. Maulbetsch (1921–28), Lynn O. Waldorf (1929–33), Albert A. Exedine (1934–35), Ted Cox (1936–38), Jim Lookabaugh (1939–49), J.B. Whitworth (1950–54), Cliff Speegle (1955–62), Phil Cutchin (1963–68), Floyd Gass (1969–71), Dave Smith (1972), Jim Stanley (1973–78), Jimmy Johnson (1979–83), Pat Jones (1984–94), Bob Simmons (1995–).

Athletic directors and their tenure: Ed Gallagher (1920–31), Lynn Waldorf (1932–33), Henry P. Iba (1935–69), Floyd Gass (1970–77), Richard A. Young (1978–82), Myron Roderick (1983–90), Jim Garner (1991–94), Terry Don Phillips (1995–).

The official logo for Oklahoma State University

UNIVERSITY OF OREGON
Eugene, Oregon

Autzen Stadium (1967)

Named for Thomas J. Autzen, Portland lumberman, sportsman, and philanthropist and founder of the Autzen Foundation.

Lights: Yes. **Seating capacity:** 41,698. **Location:** Off campus. **Playing surface:** Omniturf (artificial). **Special features:** MegaVision video scoreboard (four-color), indoor practice facility, 10 skyboxes, and 425 single seats in skybox amphitheater. **Other uses:** Local high school teams play here weekly during football season, frequent marching band competitions.

Original construction: 1966, at a cost of $2.5 million financed by private donations. **Additions and renovations:** In 1981 the Stadium Club was constructed behind the east end zone. This club has provided the team with meeting facilities and the Athletic Department with functional surroundings for pre-game functions. Lights were installed in 1999. Cost of these improvements was not reported. Sources of funds for them were private donations and athletic department monies. **Projected additions:** Plans are to add between 10–20,000 seats in another upper tier within the next two years. No cost estimate was given for this expansion.

Team name: Ducks. **Team mascot:** Duck (costumed figure). **Colors:** Lemon yellow and emerald green. **Song:** "Mighty Oregon." **Conference:** Pac-10. **First intercollegiate football game:** 1894.

Coaches and their tenure: Jerry Frei (1967–71), Dick Enright (1972–73), Don Read (1974–76), Rich Brooks (1977–94), Mike Bellotti (1995–).

Athletic directors and their tenure: Len Casanova (1967–70), Norv Ritchey (1971–76), John Caine (1977–81), Rick Bay (1982–84), Bill Byrne (1985–92), Rich Brooks (1993–94), Dan Williams (1995), Bill Moos (1996–).

University of Oregon Duck

OREGON STATE UNIVERSITY
Corvallis, Oregon

Parker Stadium (1953)

Named for Charles T. Parker, OSU alumnus, businessman, and football program benefactor.

Lights: Yes. *Seating capacity:* 35,362. *Location:* On campus. *Playing surface:* Natural grass. *Special features:* Locker rooms, two-level press box, and 13 skybox suites. *Other uses:* Occasional concerts.

Original construction: 1953, cost not reported. *Additions and renovations:* Valley Football Center, a three-story complex in north end zone, was constructed in 1990. It includes a locker room, training room, equipment room, weight room, and offices for the coaching staff. In 1996 the center was remodeled and expanded. A Jumbotron was installed in 1997. Cost of this improvement was $11.3 million. It was financed by private donations and Athletic Department funds. *Projected additions:* Expansion of seating capacity, completion of a brick wall encircling the stadium, additional field lighting, and additional concession booths and rest rooms. Estimated cost of these improvements was not reported.

Team name: Beavers. *Team mascot:* Benny Beaver (costumed figure). *Colors:* Orange and black. *Song:* "OSU Fight Song." *Conference:* Pac-10. *First intercollegiate football game:* 1893.

Coaches and their tenure: Kip Taylor (1953–54), Tommy Prothro (1955–64), Dee Andros (1965–75), Craig Fertig (1976–79), Joe Avezzano (1980–84), Dave Kragthorpe (1985–90), Jerry Pettibone (1991–96), Mike Riley (1997–).

Athletic directors and their tenure: R.S. "Spec" Keene, (1953–64), "Slats" Gill (1965–66), Jim Barratt (1967–76), Dee Andros (1977–85), Lynn Snyder (1986–90), Dutch Baughman (1991–97), Mitch Barnhart (1998–).

Benny Beaver

PENNSYLVANIA STATE UNIVERSITY
University Park, Pennsylvania

Beaver Stadium (1960)

Named for James A. Beaver, former Pennsylvania governor and president of the Penn State Board of Trustees.

Lights: Yes. **Seating capacity:** 93,967. **Location:** On campus. **Playing surface:** Grass. **Special features:** Locker rooms, luxury seats, press box. **Other uses:** None.

Original construction: 1960, cost not reported, nor was method of financing construction. **Additions and renovations:** Seats were added in each of the following years to bring seating capacity to 83,770: 1969, 1972, 1976, 1978, and 1980. In 1991 an upper deck was added to the north end zone to bring capacity to its current figure. Lights were installed in 1984. Cost of the 1978 addition was $4.93 million. The installation of lights cost was $575,000, and the 1991 addition costs $11.2 million. Revenue from the sale of tickets, private donations, and leasing of skyboxes financed these improvements. **Projected additions:** During the period 2000-2001 6,000 general seats and 4,000 club seats will be added in the south end zone, increasing the seating capacity to 103,500. During that same period 58 enclosed suites in a three-level pavilion will be added behind the east stands. Sources of revenue to finance these additions will be ticket sales revenue, private donations, and leasing of skyboxes.

Team name: Nittany Lions. **Team mascot:** Nittany Lion (costumed figure). **Colors:** Blue and white. **Song:** "Fight On State." **Conference:** Big Ten. **First intercollegiate football game:** 1887.

Coaches and their tenure: Rip Engle (1960-65), Joe Paterno (1966-).

Athletic directors and their tenure: Ernest McCoy (1960-68), Ed Czekaj (1969-80), Joe Paterno (1981-82), Jim Tarman (1983-93), Tim Curley (1994-).

Nittany Lion

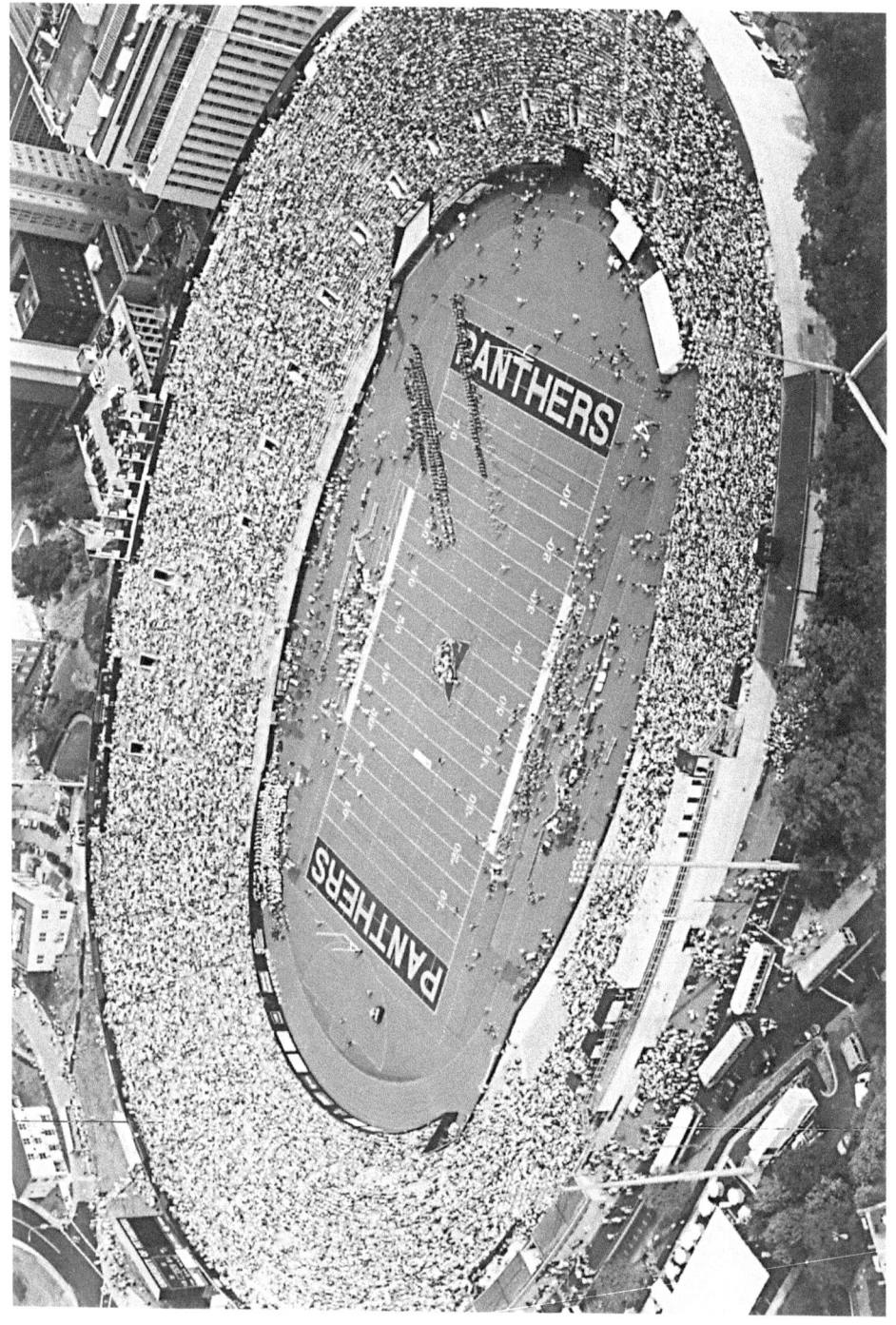

UNIVERSITY OF PITTSBURGH
Pittsburgh, Pennsylvania

Pitt Stadium (1925)

Lights: Yes. *Seating capacity:* 56,150. *Location:* On campus. *Playing surface:* Astroturf. *Special features:* Duratz Athletic Complex, coaches' offices, video suite, Athletic Department and University Band offices. *Other uses:* men and women's soccer games and track meets.

Original construction: 1925, at a cost of $2,100,000. *Additions and renovations:* In 1970 metal benches replaced wooden seats. The coaches' complex opened in 1978. The following year the ticket office opened. Lights were installed in 1986 and the Duratz Complex, an athletic training facility with home team locker rooms, opened in 1995. Construction of the Duratz Complex costs $5.87 million and was financed through the issuance of mortgage bonds, private donations, and state funds. Early in 2000 Pitt Stadium was demolished. Beginning with the 2000 season the Panthers will use Three Rivers Stadium, an off-campus facility, as their home stadium.

Team name: Panthers. *Team mascot:* Panther (costumed figure). *Colors:* Blue and gold. *Song:* "Hail to Pitt." *Conference:* Big East. *First intercollegiate football game:* 1890.

Coaches and their tenure: Dr. John B. "Jock" Sutherland (1925–38), Charles Bowser (1939–42), Clark D. Shaughnessy (1943–45), Wesley E. Fesler (1946), Walter S. Milligan (1947–49), Leonard J. Casanova (1950), Tom Hamilton (1951), Lowell P. "Red" Dawson (1952–53), Tom Hamilton (1954), John P. Michelosen (1955–65), David R. Hart (1966–68), Carl A. DePasqua (1969–72), John Majors (1973–76), Jackie Sherrill (1977–81), Serafino "Foge" Fazio (1982–85), Mike Gottfried (1986–89), Sal Sunseri (1992), John Majors (1993–96), Walt Harris (1997–).

Athletic directors and their tenure: K.E. Davis (1925–28), W. Don Harrison (1929–37), James Hagan (1938–48), Capt. Tom Hamilton (1949–59), Frank F. Carver (1960–67), Casimir J. Myslinski (1968–81), Dr. Edward J. Bozik (1982–90), L. Oval Jaynes (1991–95), Steven C. Pederson (1996–).

The Pittsburgh Panther

PURDUE UNIVERSITY
West Lafayette, Indiana

Ross-Ade Stadium (1924)

Named for David E. Ross, late president of the Purdue University Board of Trustees who conceived the idea for the stadium and selected its site, and George Ade, late writer, humorist, and Purdue alumnus.

Lights: No. *Seating capacity:* 67,332. *Location:* On campus. *Playing surface:* Prescription athletic turf (grass). *Special features:* Locker rooms, three-tier press box with elevator, Jumbotron with instant replay. *Other uses:* None.

Original construction: 1924, cost not reported. *Additions and renovations:* Seating capacity was expanded in 1949, 1955, and 1964. An elevator was added to sound end of press box in 1984. The following year a visitor locker room was constructed. In 1989 the press box was enlarged to seat 136 members of the news media. An electronic scoreboard and message center were added in 1990. Seven years later the Jumbotron was retrofitted into the main scoreboard. The 1990 improvements cost $1 million, with the 1997 improvement costing $3 million. No costs were reported for other improvements. Game ticket price increases, TV and bowl game revenue, and private donations financed the cost of all additions and renovations. *Projected additions:* Sometime early in the 21st century a new press box will replace the existing one, rest rooms and concession areas will be renovated, and a new façade as well as new entrances will be built. No cost estimate has been projected for these improvements, nor has method of financing cost been reported.

Team name: Boilermakers. *Team mascot:* Boilermaker Special. *Colors:* Black and old gold. *Song:* "Hail Purdue." *Conference:* Big Ten. *First intercollegiate football game:* 1887.

Coaches and their tenure: James M. Phelan (1924–29), Noble E. Kizer (1930–36), A.H. Mal Elward (1937–41), Elmer H. Burnham (1942–43), Cecil Isbell (1944–46), Stuart Holcomb (1947–55), Jack Mollenkopf (1956–69), Bob Demoss (1970–72), Alex Agase (1973–76), Jim Young (1977–81), Leon Burtnett (1982–86), Fred Akers (1987–90), Jim Colletto (1991–96), Joe Tiller (1997–).

Athletic directors and their tenure: N.A. Kellogg (1924–30), Noble E. Kizer (1931–36), R.C. Woodworth (1937), Noble E. Kizer (1938–39), E.C. Elliott (1940), A.H. Elward (1941), Guy J. Mackey (1942–71), George S. King, Jr. (1971–92), John W. Hicks (1993), Mogan J. Burke (1994–).

Boilermaker logo

RICE UNIVERSITY
Houston, Texas

Rice Stadium (1950)

Lights: Yes. *Seating capacity:* 70,000. *Location:* On campus. *Playing surface:* Astroturf. *Special features:* Locker rooms, three-level press box, coaches' offices, state-of-the-art scoreboard and message center, John L. Cox Fitness Center (strength and conditioning complex), and Owl Club (museum of great Rice athletes and teams). *Other uses:* Concerts. Stadium has been the site of Bluebonnet Bowl and was the site of Super Bowl VIII in 1974.

Original construction: 1950, cost not reported. *Additions and renovations:* New lights were installed in 1995, scoreboards and message centers in 1996, and a new playing surface was laid in 1997. Sports medicine and equipment areas were renovated in 1996. Cost of these improvements was not reported, nor was the method of financing used. *Projected additions:* Refurbishing public areas, including restrooms and concessions, is planned in the near future. Estimated cost of these renovations was not reported, nor was method of financing it.

Team name: Owls. *Team mascot:* Sammy the Owl (costumed figure). *Colors:* Blue and gray. *Song:* "Fight for Rice." *Conference:* Western Athletic. *First intercollegiate football game:* 1912.

Coaches and their tenure: Jess Neely (1950–66), Harold "Bo" Hogan (1967–70), Bill Peterson (1971), Al Conover (1972–75), Homer Rice (1976–77), Ray Alborn (1978–83), Watson Brown (1984–85), Jerry Berndt (1986–88), Fred Goldsmith (1989–93), Ken Hatfield (1994–).

Athletic directors and their tenure: The first athletic director was appointed in 1966. "Bo" Hogan (1966–70), Bill Peterson (1971–72), Red Bale (1973–75), Homer Rice (1976–77), Augie Erfurth (1978–84), Watson Brown (1985–86), Jerry Berndt (1987–88), Bobby May (1989–).

Sammy the Owl

RUTGERS UNIVERSITY
New Brunswick, New Jersey

Rutgers Stadium (1994)

The new Rutgers Stadium replaced the old one built in 1938.

Lights: Yes. *Seating capacity:* 41,500. *Location:* On campus. *Playing surface:* Grass. *Special features:* Two-level press box seating 125 news media personnel, two upper decks, each seating 5,000, eight concession stands, and Hale Center, a comprehensive facility which includes a locker room, coaches' offices, state-of-the-art weight room and training area. *Other uses:* Stadium was site of NCAA Division I-A lacrosse championship in 1998.

Original construction: 1938, at a cost of $1,234,707. The old stadium was financed with WPA (Federal agency) funds. Cost of the new stadium was not reported; a bond issue administered by the New Jersey Sports and Exposition Authority financed it.

Team name: Scarlet Knights. *Team mascot:* Scarlet Knight (costumed figure riding a spirited white charger). *Colors:* Scarlet and white. *Song:* "Rutgers Fight Song." *Conference:* Big East. *First intercollegiate football game:* 1869. This was the year of the nation's first intercollegiate football game between Rutgers and Princeton. Rutgers was the victor by a score of 6–4.

Coaches and their tenure: Doug Graber (1994–95), Terry Shea (1996–).

Athletic directors and their tenure: Fred Gruninger (1994–97), Bob Mulcahy (1998–).

Scarlet Knight

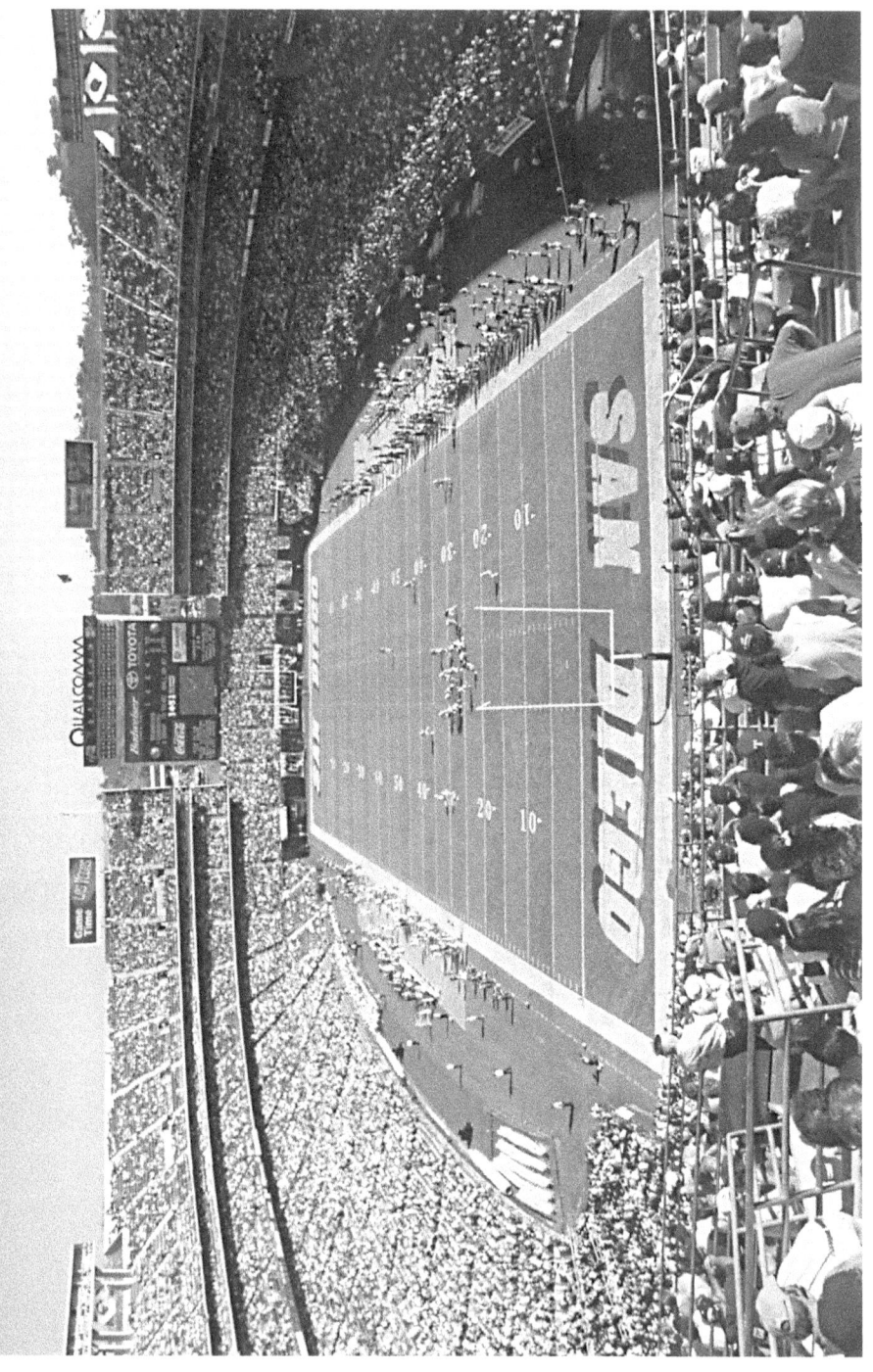

SAN DIEGO STATE UNIVERSITY
San Diego, California

Qualcomm Stadium (1967)

Named for the Qualcomm Communications Corporation, a company that paid for stadium naming rights.

Lights: Yes. **Seating capacity:** 71,400. **Location:** Off campus. **Playing surface:** Grass. **Special features:** Locker rooms, two video replay scoreboards, club seating areas, and skyboxes. **Other uses:** Soccer games, concerts, and home field for the San Diego Padres (professional baseball team) and San Diego Chargers (professional football team).

Original construction: 1967, at a cost of $27 million. **Additions and renovations:** Seating capacity was expanded in both 1985 and 1997 to host the Super Bowls played here in those two years. Club areas were enlarged and a second scoreboard was added in 1997. Cost of the 1985 addition was $9.1 million. Cost of the 1997 improvements was $66.4 million. Both of these costs were financed by the issuance of city bonds and revenue from Qualcomm rights.

Team name: Aztecs. **Team mascot:** Monty Montezuma, a costumed Aztec Indian. **Colors:** Scarlet and black. **Song:** "Fight On." **Conference:** Mountain West. **First intercollegiate football game:** 1921.

Coaches and their tenure: Don Coryell (1967–72), Claude Gilbert (1973–80), Doug Scovil (1981–85), Denny Stolz (1986–88), Al Luginbill (1989–93), Ted Tollner (1994–).

Athletic directors and their tenure: Al Olsen (1967–68), O. Ken Karr, Jr. (1969–79), Gene Bourdet (1980–83), Mary Alice Hill (1984–85), Fred Miller (1986–94), Rick Bay (1995–).

Monty Montezuma

SAN JOSE STATE UNIVERSITY
San Jose, California

Spartan Stadium (1933)

Lights: Yes. ***Seating capacity:*** 30,578. ***Location:*** Off campus. ***Playing surface:*** Grass. ***Special features:*** Locker rooms, 12 luxury boxes, computerized scoreboard. ***Other uses:*** College and professional soccer games, commencement exercises, concerts and other types of stage shows.

Original construction: 1932, cost not reported. ***Additions and renovations:*** In 1978 a new press box was built and 4,200 seats were added. Seven years later an additional 8,500 seats were installed. Cost of these improvements was not reported; however, this cost was financed through the revenue from the sale of tickets to Spartan games.

Team name: Spartans. ***Team mascot:*** Spartan. ***Colors:*** Gold, white, and blue. ***Song:*** "Spartan Fight Song." ***Conference:*** Western Athletic. ***First intercollegiate football game:*** 1893.

Coaches and their tenure: Dudley S. DeGroot (1933–39), Ben Winkleman (1940–41), Tiny Hartranft (1942), Bill Hubbard (1946–49), Bob Bronzan (1950–56), Bob Titchenal (1957–64), Harry Anderson (1965–68), Joe McMullen (1969–70), Dewey King (1971–72), Darryl Rogers (1973–75), Lynn Stiles (1976–78), Jack Elway (1979–83), Claude Gilbert (1984–89), Terry Shea (1990–91), Ron Turner (1992), John Ralston (1993–96), Dave Baldwin (1997–).

Athletic directors and their tenure: The first two men to hold this position had the title Mens' Physical Education Director. H.C. McDonald (1933–37), Dudley DeGroot (1938–39), Tiny Hartranft (1940–50), Bill Hubbard (1951–59), Walt McPherson (1960), Bob Bronzan (1961–72), John Caine (1973–76), Bob Murphy (1977– 78), Dave Adams (1979–84), Randy Hoffman (1985–89), Tom Brennan (1990–97), Chuck Bell (1998–).

Spartan logo

UNIVERSITY OF SOUTH CAROLINA
Columbia, South Carolina

Williams-Brice Stadium (1934)

Named for Martha Williams and Thomas Brice. Mr. Brice was a Gamecock football letterman from 1922 to 1924.

Lights: Yes. *Seating capacity:* 82,500. *Location:* Off campus. *Playing surface:* Natural grass. *Special features:* Press box atop west upper deck, scoreboard with video display, 15 luxury boxes, football office complex. *Other uses:* University-wide meetings, concerts, high school football championships, and occasional banquets in luxury boxes.

Original construction: 1934, cost not reported. *Additions and renovations:* Construction of east upper deck in 1982. Expansion of south end zone and building coaches' offices overlooking stadium in north end zone in 1996. Cost of these improvements was $4 million. Private donations by Gamecock Booster Club members and revenue from sale of tickets to home games financed these improvements.

Team name: Fighting gamecocks. *Team mascot:* Cocky (replaced his father Big Spur as mascot in 1980). *Colors:* Garnet and black. *Song:* "Step to the Rear." *Conference:* Southeastern. *First intercollegiate football game:* 1892.

Coaches and their tenure: Billy Caval (1934), Don McCallister (1935–37), Rex Enright (1938–42), J.P. Moran (1943), William Newton (1944), Johnnie McMillan (1945), Rex Enright (1946–55), Warren Grese (1956–60), Marvin Bass (1961–65), Paul Dietzel (1966–74), Jim Carlen (1975–81), Richard Bell (1982), Joe Morrison (1983–88), Sparky Woods (1989–93), Brad Scott (1994–98), Lou Holtz (1999–).

Athletic directors and their tenure: The Director of Student Activities supervised intercollegiate athletics until 1940, when the athletic director assumed this responsibility. Ralph K. Foster (1934–35), William H. Harth (1936–39), Rex Enright (1940–65), Paul Dietzel (1966–74), Jim Carlen (1975–81), Bob Marcum (1982–88), King Dixon (1989–91), Mike McGee (1992–).

University of Southern California
Los Angeles, California

Los Angeles Memorial Coliseum (1923)

This coliseum has been designated as a state and federal historic landmark.
Lights: Yes. **Seating capacity:** 92,000. **Location:** Off campus (in Exposition Park). **Playing surface:** Grass. **Special features:** Locker rooms, press box. Except for seats in the east end zone and the Peristyle, all seats in the stadium are individual theater-type. **Other uses:** Track meets, baseball and soccer games, concerts. Super Bowls I (1967) and VII (1973) were played here and track and field events in the 1932 and 1984 Summer Olympic Games were held here.

Original construction: 1921–23, at a cost of $955,000. Funds for construction were provided by 14 banks. **Additions and renovations:** In 1979 a scoreboard was erected, theater-type seats were installed, and concession stands were remodeled. In 1993 8,000 seats were added, the running track was removed, and locker rooms and public rest rooms were upgraded. In 1994 extensive renovation of the stadium was undertaken to repair damage caused by a strong earthquake in January of that year. The following year a new press box was built. Cost of these improvements was as follows: 1979—$9.5 million, 1993—$15 million, 1994—$93 million, 1995—$6 million. Cost of these improvements was financed by issuance of bonds and corporate gifts. **Projected additions:** Some renovation is possible if a professional football team returns to Los Angeles.

Team name: Trojans. **Team mascot:** Traveler (a live horse). **Colors:** Cardinal and gold. **Song:** "Fight On." **Conference:** Pac-10. **First intercollegiate football game:** 1888.

Coaches and their tenure: Elmer C. "Gloomy Gus" Henderson (1923–24), Howard H. Jones (1925–40), Justin M. "Sam" Barry (1941), Newell J. Cravath (1942–50), Jesse T. "Jess" Hill (1951–56), Don R. Clark (1957–59), John McKay (1960–75), John Robinson (1976–82), Ted Tollner (1983–86), Larry Smith (1987–92), John Robinson (1993–97), Paul Hackett (1998–).

Athletic directors and their tenure: Willis O. Hunter (1926–57), Jess Hill (1958–72), John McKay (1973–75), Richard Perry (1976–84), Mike McGee (1985–93), Mike Garrett (1994–).

Traveler

SOUTHERN METHODIST UNIVERSITY
Dallas, Texas

Gerald J. Ford Stadium (2000)

Named for Gerald J. Ford, recipient of two degrees from SMU, a member of the SMU Board of Trustees, and CEO of the California Federal Bank.

Lights: Yes. **Seating capacity:** 31,470. **Location:** On campus. **Playing surface:** Grass. **Special features:** 600 club level seats and 23 luxury suites as well as a three-level press box. The Paul B. Loyd, Jr. All Sports Center is a three-story building connected to the stadium. It houses all athletic locker rooms, team meeting rooms, coaches' offices, athletic department offices, a sports medicine complex, and the Altshuler Learning Enhancement Center. ATMs are located throughout the stadium. Stadium architecture is consistent with the Collegiate-Georgian style of the entire campus. **Other uses:** Soccer games.

Original construction: 2000, at a cost of $58 million. Cost was financed with private donations. The Cotton Bowl was used as the SMU home stadium during the period 1995–99. **Projected additions:** None planned.

Team name: Mustangs. **Team mascot:** Peruna, a live Shetland pony. **Colors:** Red and blue. **Song:** "Pony Battle Cry." **Conference:** Western Athletic. **First intercollegiate football game:** 1915.

Coaches and their tenure: Mike Cavan (2000—).

Athletic directors and their tenure: Jim Copeland (2000–).

"Peruna," mascot of Southern Methodist University

University of Southern Mississippi
Hattiesburg, Mississippi

M.M. Roberts Stadium (1976)

Named for Dr. M.M. Roberts, former member of the Board of Trustees, State Institutions of Higher Learning, who is credited with the development of USM as a comprehensive university.

Lights: Yes. *Seating capacity:* 33,000. *Location:* On campus. ***Playing surface:*** Natural grass, with underground irrigation system. ***Special features:*** Press box, locker rooms, limited Eagle Club chairback seating in both east and west stands. ***Other uses:*** Student functions, marching band competitions, and occasional concerts.

Original construction: 1976, at a cost of $6.3 million. ***Additions and renovations:*** In 1989 a new irrigation system was installed and seating for handicapped was added. Construction of stadium was financed with State Building Commission funds and stadium tax. ***Projected additions:*** A new visitor dressing room is planned for construction at some future date, but a target date has not been set. Cost of this project has not been determined.

Team name: Golden Eagles. ***Team mascot:*** Golden eagle represented by Seymour, a costumed figure. ***Colors:*** Black and gold. ***Song:*** "Southern to the Top." ***Conference:*** USA. ***First intercollegiate football game:*** 1912.

Coaches and their tenure: Bobby Collins (1976–81), Jim Carmody (1982–87), Curley Hallman (1988–90), Jeff Bower (1991–).

Athletic directors and their tenure: Roland Dale (1976–85), Bill McLellan (1986–).

Seymour the Golden Eagle

University of Southwestern Louisiana
Lafayette, Louisiana

Cajun Field (1971)

Lights: Yes. *Seating capacity:* 31,000. *Location:* On campus. *Playing surface:* Grass. *Special features:* Two-level press box with camera deck and seven private boxes. USL Athletic Complex houses spacious weight room and other training facilities for athletes. The stadium is also known as "The Swamp" because the playing field is set two feet below sea level in a natural bowl. With its surrounding bayous and wetlands area "The Swamp" is indeed an appropriate name. *Other uses:* Not reported.

Original construction: 1971, cost not reported. *Note:* No information was reported relating to additions, renovations, or cost thereof.

Team name: Ragin' Cajuns. *Team mascot:* Ragin' Cajuns. *Colors:* Vermilion and white. *Song:* "Fight On Cajuns." *Conference:* Independent. *First intercollegiate football game:* 1908.

Coaches and their tenure: Russ Faulkinberry (1971–73), Augie Tammariello (1974–79), Sam Robertson (1980–85), Nelson Stokley (1986–98), Jerry Baldwin (1999–).

Athletic directors and their tenure: Athletic directors during the period 1971–92 were not available. Nelson Schexnayder (1993–).

Logo for the Ragin' Cajuns

STANFORD UNIVERSITY
Stanford, California

Stanford Stadium (1921)

Lights: Yes. *Seating capacity:* 85,500. *Location:* On campus. *Playing surface:* Mixture of rye and Bermuda grass. *Special features:* Locker rooms and press box. Stadium is the largest privately owned college football facility in the United States. *Other uses:* Major events here have been the Summer Olympics soccer matches in 1984, Super Bowl XIX in 1985, and World Cup soccer competition in 1994. Republican presidential nominee Herbert Hoover delivered his acceptance speech here on August 12, 1928.

Original construction: 1921, at a cost of $200,000. Alumni subscriptions and gate receipts from the 1921 Stanford-California game financed cost of construction. *Additions and renovations:* 10,200 seats were added in 1925. Two years later an additional 14 rows of seats were erected. A press box was built in 1960. North and south end zone scoreboards were installed in 1978, and in 1985 new locker rooms, officials' dressing rooms, and additional rest rooms were constructed. Cost of these improvements was not reported, nor was the method of financing this cost.

Team name: Cardinal. *Team mascot:* None. *Colors:* Cardinal and white. *Song:* "All Right Now." *Conference:* Pac-10. *First intercollegiate football game:* 1891.

Coaches and their tenure: C.E. Van Gent (1921), Andrew Kerr (1922–23), Glenn "Pop" Warner (1924–32), C.E. Thornhill (1933–39), Clark Shaughnessy (1940–41), Marchmont Schwartz (1942, 1946–50), Charles A. Taylor (1951–57), Jack C. Curtice (1958–62), John Ralston (1963–71), Jack Christiansen (1972–76), Bill Walsh (1977–78), Rod Dowhower (1979), Paul Wiggin (1980–83), Jack Elway (1984–88), Dennis Green (1989–91), Bill Walsh (1992–94), Tyrone Willingham (1995–).

Athletic directors and their tenure: Al Masters (1925–63), Chuck Taylor (1964–71), Joe Ruetz (1972–78), Andy Geiger (1979–91), Ted Leland (1992–).

Logo for Stanford University

SYRACUSE UNIVERSITY
Syracuse, New York

Carrier Dome (1980)

Named for the Carrier Corporation, which donated $2.75 million to help finance cost of dome construction.

Lights: Yes. *Seating capacity:* 49,900. *Location:* On campus. *Playing surface:* Astroturf (removable). *Special features:* Five locker rooms, press box seating 130 members of news media, 38 luxury boxes, first-aid room, and seating for the disabled. Stadium is reportedly the only on-campus domed facility in the nation. Ernie Davis Room houses an Athletic Department display case and museum. Orange Pack Room is used for meetings, luncheons, and dinners. *Other uses:* Commencement exercises, concerts, track and field events, and basketball, lacrosse, and soccer games.

Original construction: 1979, at a cost of $28 million. A state grant and private donations, including a gift from Carrier Corporation, financed construction cost. *Additions and renovations:* A new roof was placed on the Dome in 1999. Cost of this improvement was not reported, nor was the method of financing it.

Team name: Orangemen. *Team mascot:* Otto the Orange (costumed figure). *Colors:* Orange and white. *Song:* "Down, Down the Field." *Conference:* Big East. *First intercollegiate football game:* 1889.

Coaches and their tenure: Frank Maloney (1980), Dick MacPherson (1981–90), Paul Pasqualoni (1991–).

Athletic directors and their tenure: Jake Crouthamel (1980–).

Otto the Orange

TEMPLE UNIVERSITY
Philadelphia, Pennsylvania

Veterans Stadium (1971)

Veterans Stadium is a part of the Sports Complex which comprises John F. Kennedy Stadium, First Union Center (an indoor arena), and Veterans Stadium. The stadium is owned and operated by the City of Philadelphia. The Temple Owls played their first home game here in 1974.

Lights: Yes. *Seating capacity:* 65,352. *Location:* Off campus. *Playing surface:* Astroturf. *Special features:* Press box, 89 luxury suites, animated scoreboard, and video boards. The Athletic Complex on the Temple campus houses strength and conditioning and physical training facilities. Near this complex are two practice football fields. *Other uses:* The Philadelphia Eagles, a professional football team, and the Philadelphia Phillies, a major league baseball team, play their home games here. Each December the Army-Navy game is played on this site.

Original construction: 1968, at a cost of $50 million. This cost was financed with bonds issued by the City of Philadelphia. *Additions and renovations:* Since 1985 approximately $74 million has been spent for structural repairs, seat additions, replacement of old elevators, a lighting system upgrade, and other improvements. The method of financing this cost was not reported.

Team name: Owls. *Team mascot:* The Owl (a costumed figure). *Colors:* Cherry and white. *Song:* "Temple Fight Song." *Conference:* Big East. *First intercollegiate football game:* 1894.

Coaches and their tenure: Wayne Hardin (1974–82), Bruce Arions (1983–88), Jerry Berndt (1989–92), Ron Dickerson (1993–97), Bobby Wallace (1998–).

Athletic directors and their tenure: Ernest Casale (1974–81), Gavin White (1982–85), Charlie Theokas (1986–92), Jim Brown (1993), R.C. Johnson (1994–95), Dave O'Brien (1996–).

The Temple University Owl

UNIVERSITY OF TENNESSEE
Knoxville, Tennessee

Neyland Stadium (1921)

Named for General Robert R. Neyland, head football coach at UT for 18 years and athletic director there for 29 years.

Lights: Yes. **Seating capacity:** 102,854 (the second largest seating capacity of any college football stadium in the United States). **Location:** On campus. **Playing surface:** Grass. **Special features of stadium:** Locker rooms, press box, 42 luxury suites. **Other uses:** None.

Original construction: 1919, cost not reported, nor was method of financing cost. **Additions and renovations:** Since 1926 the seating capacity has been increased 12 times. The most recent expansion was the addition of the north upper deck – 10,952 seats – in 1996. **Projected additions:** Construction of additional luxury suites and installation of Jumbotron video screens is planned, but no completion date has been set. The source of funds for all additions has been private donations and fund-raising campaigns. Cost of these expansions was not reported.

Team name: Volunteers. **Team mascot:** Smokey, a live blue tick hound dog. **Colors:** Orange and white. **Song:** "Down the Field." **Conference:** Southeastern. **First intercollegiate football game:** 1891.

Coaches and their tenure: M.B. Banks (1921–25), R.R. Neyland (1926–34), W.H. Britton (1935), John Barnhill (1941–45), R.R. Neyland (1946–52), Harvey Robinson (1953–54), Bowden Wyatt (1955–62), Jim McDonald (1963), Doug Dickey (1964–69), Bill Battle (1970–76), Johnny Majors (1977–92), Phillip Fulmer (1992–).

Athletic directors and their tenure: R.R. Neyland (1926–34), Paul B. Parker (1935), R.R. Neyland (1936–40), John Barnhill (1941–45), R.R. Neyland (1946–62), Robert Woodruff (1963–85), Doug Dickey (1986–).

Smokey

UNIVERSITY OF TEXAS–AUSTIN
Austin, Texas

Darrell K. Royal–Texas Memorial Stadium (1924)

Named for Darrell K. Royal, who was the Longhorns' head football coach for two decades and led the team to three national championships during this period. Stadium is also named in honor of more than 198,000 Texans who fought in World War I.

Lights: Yes. *Seating capacity:* 80,216. *Location:* On campus. *Playing surface:* Natural grass. *Special features:* Press box, luxury suites, Sony Jumbotron, locker rooms, retrofitted scoreboard dedicated to the memory of Freddie Steinmark, Longhorn player who died of cancer in 1971, and the Moncrief-Neuhaus Athletic Complex which houses a strength and conditioning center, training center, and equipment room. *Other uses:* None. A track and soccer stadium, located east of the football stadium, was completed in 1999.

Original construction: 1924, at cost of $275,000. *Additions and renovations:* Seating capacity was enlarged to 40,500 in 1926 and again to 60,130 in 1948. Eight sets of lights were installed in 1955 and the seating capacity was increased to 77,809 in 1971. In 1998 5,000 seats were added to the upper deck on the east side. The following year the track was removed and the field lowered to accommodate 1,600 field-level seats. In 1998 a 13,000 square foot club room designed to seat 1,200 was built and 52 luxury suites were added. Cost of these improvements was approximately $20 million; the method of financing the cost was not reported.

Team name: Longhorns. *Team mascot:* Longhorn steer (live animal). *Colors:* Burnt orange and white. *Song:* "Texas Fight." *Conference:* Big 12. *First intercollegiate football game:* 1893.

Coaches and their tenure: E.J. "Doc" Stewart (1924–26), Clyde Littlefield (1927–33), Jack Chevigny (1934–36), Dana X. Bible (1937–46), Blair Cherry (1947–50), Edwin Booth Price (1951–56), Darrell K. Royal (1957–76), Fred Akers (1977–86), David McWilliams (1987–91), John Mackovic (1992–97), Mack Brown (1998–).

Athletic directors and their tenure: L. Theo Bellmont (1924–28), H.J. Ettlinger (1929–30), W.E. Metzenthin (1931–35), Jack Chevigny (1936–37), Dana X. Bible (1938–57), Ed Olle (1958–62), Darrell K. Royal (1963–79), Bill Ellington (1980–81), DeLoss Dodds (1982–).

UNIVERSITY OF TEXAS–EL PASO
El Paso, Texas

Sun Bowl (1963)

Lights: Yes. *Seating capacity:* 52,000. *Location:* On campus. *Playing surface:* Artificial turf. *Special features:* Press box, locker rooms, and Captains Club (seating for donors to UTEP athletic program). *Other uses:* Concerts, shows. The Sun Bowl game is played here the last week in December each year.

Original construction: 1960. Cost of construction not reported. Cost was financed by issuance of public bonds. *Additions and renovations:* In 1969 a second deck on the press box was erected. In 1982 the stadium was expanded by 22,000 seats. Cost of these improvements was not reported; it was financed by issuance of public bonds. No further addition or renovation is projected in the near future.

Team name: Miners. *Team mascot:* Paydirt Pete (costumed figure). *Colors:* Orange, blue, and white. *Song:* "Miners Fight." *Conference:* Western Athletic. *First intercollegiate football game:* 1914.

Coaches and their tenure: Warren Harper (1963–64), Bobby Dobbs (1965–72), Tommy Hudspeth (1973), Gil Bartosh (1974–76), Bill Michael (1977–80), Bill Alton (1981), Bill Yung (1982–85), Bob Stull (1986–88), David Lee (1989–93), Charlie Bailey (1994–).

Athletic directors and their tenure: George McCarty (1963–73), Jim Bowden (1974–82), Bill Cords (1983–87), Brad Hovious (1988–93), John Thompson (1994–97), Bob Stull (1998–).

Paydirt Pete

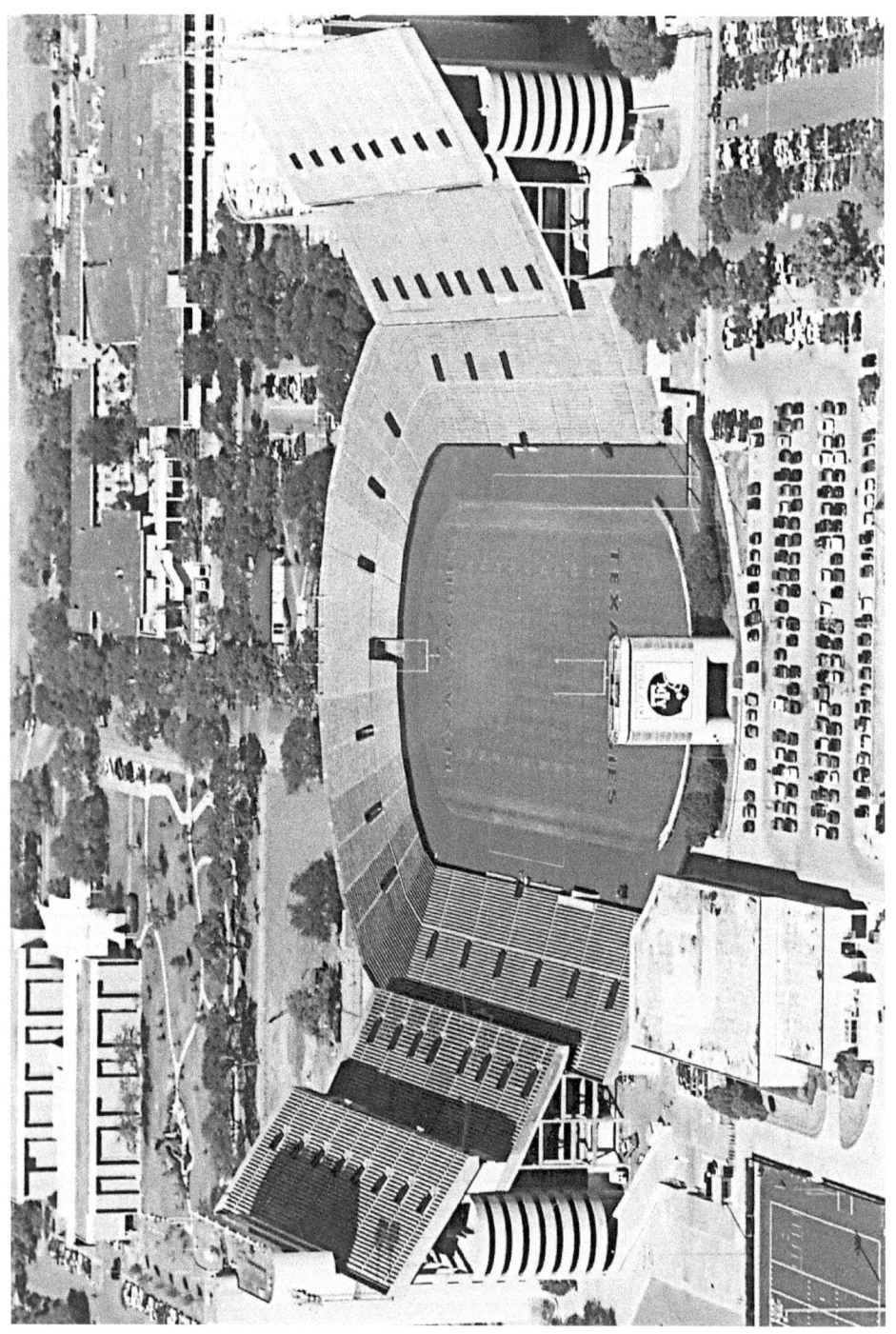

TEXAS A&M UNIVERSITY
College Station, Texas

Kyle Field (1927)

Named for Edwin Jackson Kyle, former dean of agriculture and president of the Athletic Council at Texas A&M.

Lights: Yes. **Seating capacity:** 80,000. **Location:** On campus. **Playing surface:** Natural grass. **Special features:** Locker rooms, training rooms, press box, video lab, Sony Jumbotron, 20 north end suites, 48 west side suites, and 2,000 club seats with 14,000 square foot lounge in north end. **Other uses:** None.

Original construction: 1927, at a cost of approximately $300,000. Method of financing this construction was not reported. **Additions and renovations:** Minor additions and renovations were made in 1929, 1952, and 1976–77. In 1967 a second deck was added, and in 1980 a third deck was completed. In 1998–99 12,000 old seats were demolished and replaced with 22,000 new concrete seats and 20 suites were added to the north end zone. Cost of these improvements was $38 million and was financed with donations from the 12th Man Foundation, a support group for A&M athletic programs.

Team name: Aggies. **Team mascot:** Reveille VI, a live full-bred American collie dog. **Colors:** Maroon and white. **Song:** "War Hymn." **Conference:** Big 12. **First intercollegiate football game:** 1894.

Coaches and their tenure: D.X. Bible (1927–28), Matty Bell (1929–33), Homer Norton (1934–47), Harry Stiteler (1948–50), Raymond George (1951–53), Paul Bryant (1954–57), Jim Meyers (1958–61), Hank Foldberg (1962–64), Gene Stallings (1965–71), Emory Bellard (1972–78), Tom Wilson (1979–81), Jackie Sherrill (1982–88), R.C. Slocum (1989–).

Athletic directors and their tenure: Prior to 1947 the head football coach served as athletic director. W.R. Carmichael (1947–49), Barlow Irvin (1950–53), Paul Bryant (1954–57), Barlow Irvin (1958–68), Gene Stallings (1969–71), Emory Bellard (1972–78), Marvin Tate (1979–81), Jackie Sherrill (1982–88), John David Crow (1989–92), Wally Groff (1993–).

Reveille VI, mascot of Texas A&M

TEXAS CHRISTIAN UNIVERSITY
Fort Worth, Texas

Amon G. Carter Stadium (1929)

Named after Amon G. Carter, publisher of the *Fort Worth Star-Telegram* and a renowned statesman who is generally considered to be responsible for putting both the City of Fort Worth and TCU on the national map.

Lights: Yes. **Seating capacity:** 44,008. **Location:** On campus. **Playing surface:** Natural grass. **Special features:** Locker rooms, training rooms, meeting rooms, coaches' offices, two-level press box, electronic scoreboard/message center. **Other uses:** None.

Original construction: 1929, cost not reported, nor was method of financing cost. **Additions and renovations:** In 1948 seating capacity was increased by 8,500. Three years later another addition expanded capacity to 33,000. Another 4,000 seats were added in 1953. Erection of upper deck on west side added 9,000 seats in 1956. In 1983 a new lighting system was installed and TV camera platforms were built. In 1999 an academic center housing new football offices, video and meeting rooms was constructed. That same year a heritage center was built which houses documents relating to the TCU athletic program. Cost of these improvements, which were financed by private donations, was not reported.

Team name: Horned Frogs. **Team mascot:** Super Frog (costumed figure). **Colors:** Purple and white. **Song:** None. **Conference:** Western Athletic. **First intercollegiate football game:** 1896.

Coaches and their tenure: Francis A. Schmidt (1929–33), Dutch Meyer (1934–52), Abe Martin (1953–66), Fred Taylor (1967–70), Jim Pittman (1971), Billy Tohill (1972–73), Jim Shofner (1974–76), F.A. Dry (1977–82), Jim Wacker (1983–91), Pat Sullivan (1992–97), Dennis Franchione (1998–).

Athletic directors and their tenure: Various committees (1929–33), Dutch Meyer (1934–53), Abe Martin (1954–75), Frank Windegger (1976–96), Eric Hymen (1997–).

Logo for TCU Horned Frogs

TEXAS TECH UNIVERSITY
Lubbock, Texas

Clifford B. and Audry Jones Stadium (1947)

Named for Clifford B. Jones, president of Texas Tech during the 1940s, and his wife Audry Jones.

Lights: Yes. **Seating capacity:** 50,500. **Location:** On campus. **Playing surface:** Artificial turf. **Special features:** Locker rooms, intercollegiate athletics offices, and four-level press box with club seating. **Other uses:** None.

Original construction: 1947, at a cost of $400,000. **Additions and renovations:** In 1959 41,500 seats were added to the stadium. This addition has been called an engineering feat in that railroad tracks were used to relocate the concrete stands to accommodate more seats. Cost of this addition was not reported; it was financed with University funds and private donations. **Projected additions:** A six-year renovation program will include the building of 40 luxury suites, a new press box, and modernization of locker rooms and concession stands. This program will begin when funds become available. No target date has been set for its completion.

Team name: Red Raiders. **Team mascot:** Raider Red, the masked rider (costumed figure). **Colors:** Scarlet and black. **Song:** "Fight! Raiders Fight." **Conference:** Big 12. **First intercollegiate football game:** 1947.

Coaches and their tenure: Dell Morgan (1949–50), Dewitt Weaver (1951–60), J.T. King (1961–69), Jim Carlen (1970–74), Steve Sloan (1975–77), Rex Dockery (1978–80), Jerry Moore (1981–85), David McWilliams (1986), Spike Dykes (1987–99), Mike Leach (2000–).

Athletic directors and their tenure: Morley Jennings (1947–51), Dewitt Weaver (1952–60), Polk Robison (1961–70), J.T. King (1971–78), Dick Tamburo (1979–80), John Conley (1981–85), T. Jones (1986–93), Bob Bockrath (1994–96), Gerald Myers (1997–).

Raider Red, the masked rider

UNIVERSITY OF TOLEDO
Toledo, Ohio

Glass Bowl (1937)

The City of Toledo is home to many companies which produce glass.

Lights: Yes. *Seating capacity:* 26,248. *Location:* On campus. *Playing surface:* Artificial turf. *Special features:* Locker rooms, Jumbotron. With 41 luxury suites, the press tower is one of the largest in the United States. *Other uses:* Concerts, practice facility for other intercollegiate sports on campus.

Original construction: 1937, at a cost of $272,000. Method of financing this cost was not reported. *Additions and renovations:* In 1990 a three-story press tower was constructed and new seats were added. A new digital instant replay scoreboard was installed in 1999. Cost of the 1990 improvements was $18.5 million. Cost of the scoreboard installation was approximately $750,000. In both cases, the issuance of revenue bonds financed the cost of the project.

Team name: Rockets. *Team mascot:* Rocky the Rocket (costumed figure). *Colors:* Blue and gold. *Song:* "U of Toledo." *Conference:* Mid-American. *First intercollegiate football game:* 1917.

Coaches and their tenure: Clarence "Doc" Spears (1937–42), Bill Orwig (1946–47), J.N. Stahley (1948–49), Robert Snyder (1950), Don Greenwood (1951), Clair Dunn (1952–53), Forrest England (1954–55), Jack Morton (1956), Harry Larche (1957–59), Clive Rush (1960–62), Frank Lauterbur (1963–70), Jack Murphy (1971–76), Chuck Stobart (1977–81), Dan Simrell (1982–89), Nick Saban (1990), Gary Pinkel (1991–).

Athletic directors and their tenure: Clarence Spears (1937–42), Dave Connelly (1944–50), A.G. "Barney" Francis (1951–54), Forrest England (1955–57), James W. Long (1958–63), Francis X. Lauterbur (1964–71), Vern Smith (1972–86), Allen R. Bohl (1987–95), Pete Liske (1996–).

Rocky the Rocket

TULANE UNIVERSITY
New Orleans, Louisiana

Louisiana Superdome (1975)

Lights: Yes. *Seating capacity:* 76,791. *Location:* Off campus. *Playing surface:* Artificial turf ("Mardi Grass"). *Special features:* Meeting rooms, locker rooms, private box suites, two supervision video systems, four message boards, two scoreboards which post scores for out-of-town games. *Other uses:* Commencement exercises, concerts, college and professional baseball games. The New Orleans Saints, a professional football team, plays its home games here. The NCAA Final Four basketball tournament was held here in 1982, 1987, and 1993. The Sugar Bowl is played here each January.

Original construction: 1975, at a cost of $163 million. Since the Superdome is owned and operated by the State of Louisiana, state funds financed the cost of construction. *Additions and renovations:* Additional terrace level amenities, Gate A and ticket office renovations, end zone seating modifications, meeting room refurbishing, and improvements in providing access for disabled persons. Cost of these renovations was $22 million, with state funds being used to pay for them.

Team name: Green Wave. *Team mascot:* Riptide (costumed figure). *Colors:* Olive green and sky blue. *Song:* "Tulane Fight Song." *Conference:* USA. *First intercollegiate football game:* 1893.

Coaches and their tenure: Bennie Ellender (1975), Larry Smith (1976–79), Vince Gibson (1980–82), Wally English (1983–84), Mack Brown (1985–87), Greg Davis (1988–91), Buddy Teevens (1992–96), Tommy Bowden (1997–98), Chris Scelfo (1999–).

Athletic directors and their tenure: Dr. Rix N. Yard (1975–76), Hindman Wall (1977–85), Mack Brown (1986–87), Kevin Gladchuck (1988–90), Kevin White (1991–96), Sandy Barbour (1997–).

Riptide (mascot for Tulane University)

UNIVERSITY OF TULSA
Tulsa, Oklahoma

Skelly Stadium (1930)

Named for William G. Skelly, an oil company executive and University benefactor who contributed substantially to the stadium building fund.

Lights: Yes. **Seating capacity:** 40,385. **Location:** On campus. **Playing surface:** Stadia Turf (artificial). **Special features:** Locker rooms, press box, elevator, and escalator. **Other uses:** Soccer games. In the 1970s the Knights and Mustangs, men's professional football teams, played here. The Tulsa Babes, a women's professional football team, played several games here in 1977.

Original construction: 1930, at a cost of $300,000. Method of financing this cost was not reported. **Additions and renovations:** Seating capacity was enlarged by 26,000 seats in 1965. In 1966 a photo deck was added to the press box. A modern scoreboard and animated message center was installed in 1980. Two years later a new artificial turf and lighting system were installed. In 1984 a new scoreboard was erected in the north end zone. Nine years later a new south end zone scoreboard was constructed. Cost of the 1965 addition was $1.25 million. Private donations and corporate grants financed this cost.

Team name: Golden Hurricane. **Team mascot:** Captain 'Cane (costumed figure). **Colors:** Old Gold, royal blue, and crimson. **Song:** "Hurricane Spirit." **Conference:** Western Athletic. **First intercollegiate football game:** 1895.

Coaches and their tenure: Elmer Henderson (1930–35), Vic Hurt (1936–38), Chet Benefiel (1939–40), Henry Frnka (1941–45), J.O. Brothers (1946–52), Bernie Witucki (1953–54), Bobby Dobbs (1955–60), Glenn Dobbs (1961–68), Vince Carillot (1969), Claude Gibson (1970–72), F.A. Dry (1973–76), John Cooper (1977–84), Don Morton (1985–86), George Henshaw (1987), David Rader (1988–99), Keith Burns (2000–).

Athletic directors and their tenure: Judy MacLeod (1997–). Athletic directors prior to 1997 are not available.

Captain 'Cane

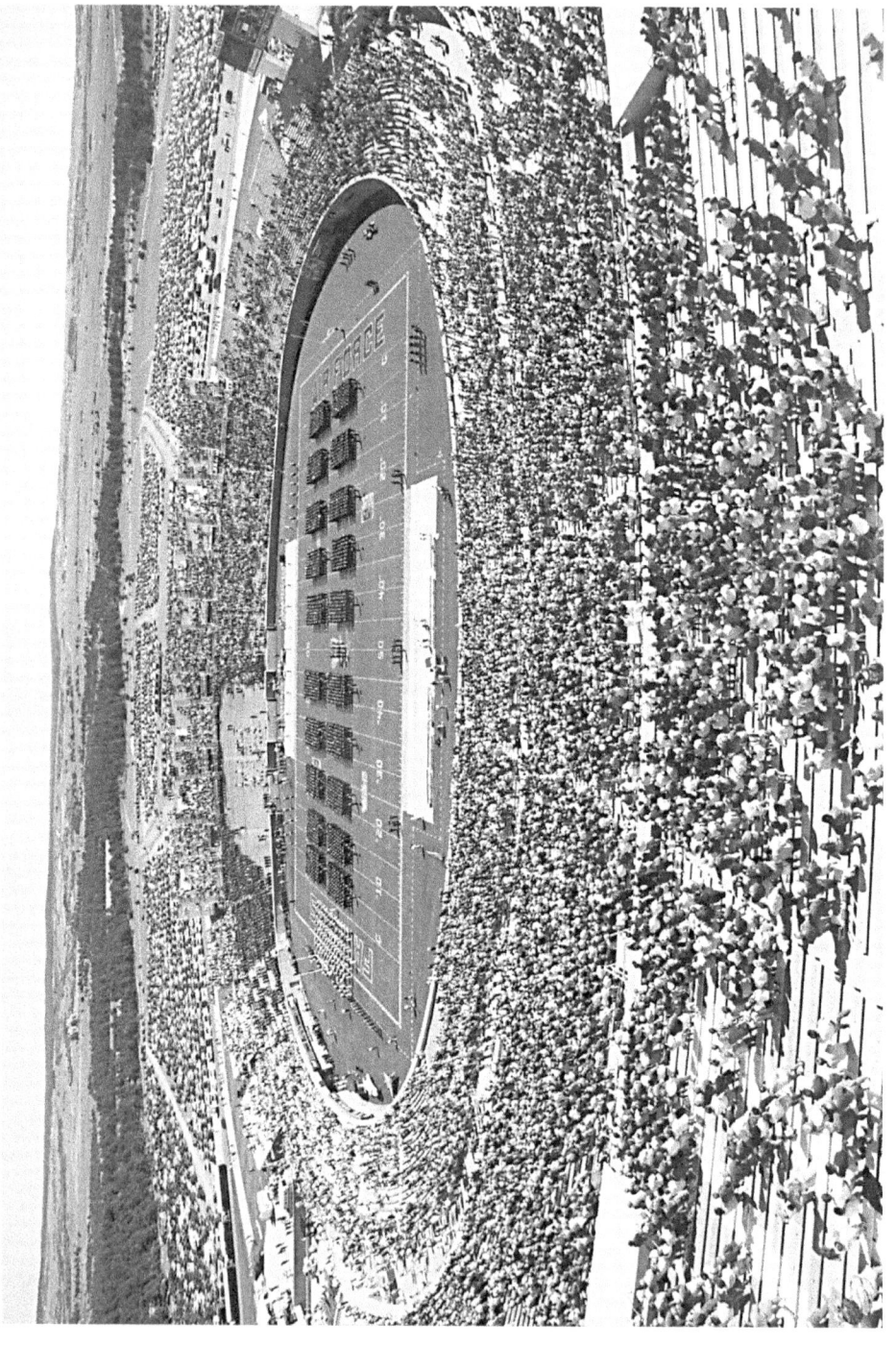

UNITED STATES AIR FORCE ACADEMY
Colorado Springs, Colorado

Falcon Stadium (1962)

Named for the falcon, mascot for all Academy athletic teams.

Lights: No. *Seating capacity:* 52,480. *Location:* On campus. *Playing surface:* Grass. *Special features:* Locker rooms, luxury boxes, and Blue-Silver Club area in the press box. This club is the support group for the Academy athletic program. *Other uses:* Commencement exercises.

Original construction: 1961, at a cost of $3.5 million. Method of financing this cost was not reported. *Additions and renovations:* In 1991 nine luxury boxes were constructed. Five years later a new message board was installed, and in 1997 natural grass replaced artificial turf. Cost of these improvements was $788,000; no method of financing this cost was reported.

Team name: Falcons. *Team mascot:* Falcon (the only live performing mascot in the NCAA). *Colors:* Blue and silver. *Song:* "Air Force Song." *Conference:* Mountain West. *First intercollegiate football game:* 1956.

Coaches and their tenure: Ben Martin (1962–77), Bill Parcells (1978), Ken Hatfield (1979–83), Fisher DeBerry (1984–).

Athletic directors and their tenure: Colonel Maurice Martin (1962–63), Colonel Edmund Rafalko (1964–67), Colonel Frank Merritt (1968–75), Colonel John Clune (1976–91), Colonel Kenny Schweitzer (1992–96), Colonel Randall Spetman (1997–).

U.S. Air Force Academy logo

UNITED STATES MILITARY ACADEMY
West Point, New York

Michie Stadium (1924)

Named for Dennis Mahan Michie, an 1892 graduate of the Academy, who organized, managed, and coached the first Academy football team in 1890.

Lights: No. **Seating capacity:** 39,929. **Location:** On campus. **Playing surface:** Artificial turf. **Special features:** Press box, coaches' offices, Superintendent's loge, weight, equipment, training, and locker rooms. **Other uses:** Commencement exercises, lacrosse games.

Original construction: 1924, no cost reported. **Additions and renovations:** Construction of permanent east stands was completed in 1962. In 1969 an upper deck on the west side was added, enlarging the seating capacity by 1,500. Different turfs were installed in 1977, 1984, and 1992. Cost of these improvements was not reported; this cost was financed by private donations.

Team name: Cadets, Black Knights. **Team mascot:** Mule (a live animal). **Colors:** Black, gold, and gray. **Song:** "On Brave Old Army Team." **Conference:** USA. Army played as an independent for 108 years before joining a conference in 1998. **First intercollegiate football game:** 1890.

Coaches and their tenure: John McEwan (1924–25), Biff Jones (1926–29), Ralph Sasse (1930–32), Gar Davidson (1933–37), William Wood (1938–40), Earl Blaik (1941–58), Dale Hall (1959–61), Paul Dietzel (1962–65), Tom Cahill (1966–73), Homer Smith (1974–78), Lou Saban (1979), Ed Cavanaugh (1980–82), Jim Young (1983–90), Bob Sutton (1991–99), Todd Berry (2000–).

Athletic directors and their tenure: The first athletic director was appointed in 1948. Earl H. Blaik (1948–58), Colonel Emory S. Adams, Jr. (1959–66), Colonel Jerry G. Capka (1967–68), Colonel August Dielens, Jr. (1969–70), Colonel William J. Schuder (1971–75), William T. Call, Jr. (1976), Raymond Murphy (1977–79), Carl Ullrich (1980–90), Al Vanderbush (1991–99), Rick Greenspan (2000–).

Army mules

UNITED STATES NAVAL ACADEMY
Annapolis, Maryland

Navy–Marine Corps Memorial Stadium (1959)

Named for everyone who has served in the U.S. Navy and Marine Corps.
Lights: Yes. *Seating capacity:* 35,000. *Location:* Off campus. *Playing surface:* Grass. *Special features:* Locker rooms, press box, and Walk of Fame, a list of all the battles fought by the U.S. Navy and Marine Corps which appears on the stadium wall. *Other uses:* Commencement exercises and lacrosse games.
Original construction: 1959, at a cost of $3 million. Private donations financed the cost of construction. *Additions and renovations:* Locker rooms and Walk of Fame were added in 1992 at a cost of $3 million, which was financed by private donations.
Team name: Midshipmen. *Team mascot:* Bill the Goat (live animal). *Colors:* Navy blue and gold. *Song:* "Anchors Aweigh." *Conference:* Independent. *First intercollegiate football game:* 1879.
Coaches and their tenure: Wayne Hardin (1959–64), Bill Elias (1965–68), Rick Forzana (1969–72), George Welsh (1973–81), Gary Tranquill (1982–86), Elliot Uzelac (1987–89), George Chaump (1990–94), Charlie Weatherbie (1995–).
Athletic directors and their tenure: Asbury Coward (1959–62), Bill Busik (1963–65), Alan Cameron (1966–68), Bo Coppedge (1969–88), Jack Lengyel (1989–).

Bill the Goat from the United States Naval Academy

UNIVERSITY OF UTAH
Salt Lake City, Utah

Rice-Eccles Stadium (1927)

Named for Robert L. Rice and Spence Eccles, both alumni and longtime supporters of the University of Utah.

Lights: Yes. *Seating capacity:* 45,634. *Location:* On campus. *Playing surface:* Sport grass (natural turf with artificial base). *Special features:* Press box, 25 luxury suites, and a 400-seat scholarship box. *Other uses:* Concerts, meetings, wedding receptions, etc., take place in a seven-story tower on one side of the stadium.

Original construction: 1927, cost not reported. *Additions and renovations:* In 1998 seating capacity was increased from 32,500 to current figure. A new press box and scholarship/suite boxes were constructed that same year. Cost of these improvements was $50 million and was financed by issuance of bonds, private donations, and Summer Olympic Games 2002 funds.

Team name: Utes. *Team mascot:* Swoop, a live red-tailed hawk. *Colors:* Crimson and white. *Song:* "Utah Man." *Conference:* Mountain West. *First intercollegiate football game:* 1892.

Coaches and their tenure: Ike Armstrong (1927–49), Jack Curtice (1950–57), Ray Nagel (1958–65), Bill Meek (1968–73), Tom Lovat (1974–76), Wayne Howard (1977–81), Chuck Stobart (1982–84), Jim Fassel (1985–89), Ron McBride (1990–).

Athletic directors and their tenure: Ike Armstrong (1927–50), Jack Curtice (1951–58), James R. "Bud" Jack (1959–76), Arnie Ferrin (1977–85), Jim Copeland (1986–87), Dr. Chris Hill (1988–).

Utes logo

UTAH STATE UNIVERSITY
Logan, Utah

Romney Stadium (1969)

Named for E.L. "Dick" Romney, head football coach at Utah State University during the period 1919–48.

Lights: Yes. *Seating capacity:* 35,257. *Location:* On campus. *Playing surface:* Grass. *Special features:* Press box, state-of-the-art locker rooms, and coaches' offices. *Other uses:* None.

Original construction: 1968. Neither cost of construction nor financing method was reported. *Additions and renovations:* 10,000 seats were added to the southern bowl in 1980. In 1997 4,000 chairback seats replaced wooden bleachers. In 1999 two new scoreboards were installed and seating capacity was increased by 5,000 in two sections of the stadium. Cost of these improvements was not reported; private donations financed this cost.

Team name: Aggies. *Team mascot:* Big Blue (costumed figure). *Colors:* Navy blue and white. *Song:* None. *Conference:* Big West. *First intercollegiate football game:* 1892.

Coaches and their tenure: Chuck Mills (1969–72), Phil Krueger (1973–75), Bruce Snyder (1976–82), Chris Pella (1983–85), Chuck Shelton (1986–91), Charlie Weatherbie (1992–94), John L. Smith (1995–97), Dave Arslanian (1998–).

Athletic directors and their tenure: Ladell Anderson (1969–82), Dave Kraigthorpe (1983–84), Rod Tueller (1985–91), Chuck Bell (1992–97), Bruce Van De Velde (1998–).

USU Aggies logo

VANDERBILT UNIVERSITY
Nashville, Tennessee

Vanderbilt Stadium (1922)

The stadium was dedicated in 1981. Prior to that year, it was named Dudley Field in memory of Dr. William Dudley, Dean of the Vanderbilt Medical College during the period 1885–1914.

Lights: Yes. *Seating capacity:* 41,448. *Location:* On campus. *Playing surface:* Natural grass (used for first time in 1999). *Special features:* Locker rooms, three-level, 17,000 square foot press box with suites and two elevators, two first-aid stations. *Other uses:* Occasional concerts, women's lacrosse games. A Billy Graham Crusade was held here in Fall 1954, and the Tennessee Oilers, a professional football team, used the stadium as a temporary home during the 1998 season.

Original construction: 1922, cost not reported. *Additions and renovations:* In 1976 new bleachers were erected in the north end zone. A modern press box was constructed and west side seats were added to increase capacity to 27,901 in 1949. In 1981, with the exception of metal stands seating 12,088, Dudley Field was demolished and replaced by Vanderbilt Stadium within a period of nine months. Cost of this 1981 project was $10.1 million. Private donations financed this cost.

Team name: Commodores. *Team mascot:* Mr. Commodore. *Colors:* Black and gold. *Song:* "Dynamite." *Conference:* Southeastern. *First intercollegiate football game:* 1890.

Coaches and their tenure: Dan McGugin (1922–34), Ray Morrison (1935–39), Red Sanders (1940–42), E.H. Alley (1943), Doby Bartling (1944–45), Red Sanders (1946–48), Bill Edwards (1949–52), Art Guepe (1953–62), Jack Green (1963–66), Bill Pace (1967–72), Steve Sloan (1973–74), Fred Pancoast (1975–78), George MacIntyre (1979–85), Watson Brown (1986–90), Gerry DiNardo (1991–94), Rod Dowhower (1995–96), Woody Widenhofer (1997–).

Athletic directors and their tenure: Prior to 1967 the head football coach acted as the athletic director. Jess Neely (1967–71), Bill Pace (1972–73), Clay Stapleton (1974–78), Roy Kramer (1979–90), Paul Hoolahan (1991–96), Todd Turner (1997–).

Mr. Commodore

UNIVERSITY OF VIRGINIA
Charlottesville, Virginia

Scott Stadium (1931)

University benefactors Frederic W. and Elizabeth S. Scott provided funds for construction of the original stadium, which was dedicated in memory of his parents Frederic Robert and Frances B. Scott.

Lights: Yes. *Seating capacity:* 60,000 with additional hillside seating. *Location:* On campus. *Playing surface:* Prescription athletic turf replaced artificial turf in 1995. *Special features:* Press box with seating capacity of 150, locker rooms, President's Box, and dining facility. Monticello Mountain serves as a backdrop, adding to the scenic view. *Other uses:* The press box is occasionally used for group gatherings. Although the stadium has been used for other athletic events in the past, it is not used for such events at present.

Original construction: 1931, at a cost of $300,000. Method of financing this cost was not reported. *Additions and renovations:* Artificial turf was installed in 1981. The previous year 12,000 seats were added to the upper level. A permanent lighting system was installed in 1983. Seating capacity was increased to current figure in 2000. That same year space for locker room and support staff facilities was doubled, a new scoreboard with instant replay capability was installed, and access for the disabled was upgraded. Estimated cost for these improvements was $50 million. This cost was financed by a $25 million challenge gift from a UVA alumnus, private donations, and other funds generated from the University.

Team name: Cavaliers, Wahoos. *Team mascot:* Cavalier (costumed figure). *Colors:* Orange and blue. *Song:* "The Good Old Song." *Conference:* Atlantic Coast. *First intercollegiate football game:* 1888.

Coaches and their tenure: Fred Dawson (1931–33), Gus Tebell (1934–36), Frank Murray (1937–45), Art Guepe (1946–52), Ned McDonald (1953–55), Ben Martin (1956–57), Richard Voris (1958–60), Bill Elias (1961–64), George Blackburn (1965–70), Don Lawrence (1971–73), Sonny Randle (1974–75), Dick Bestwick (1976–81), George Welsh (1982–).

Athletic directors and their tenure: James G. Driver (1931–35), Norton Pritchett (1936–51), Gus Tebell (1952–62), Steve Sebo (1963–70), Eugene Corrigan (1971–80), Dick Schultz (1981–87), Jim Copeland (1988–95), Terry Holland (1996–).

Cavalier

Virginia Polytechnic Institute and State University
Blacksburg, Virginia

Lane Stadium (1965)

Named for Edward H. Lane, a VPI graduate, former member of the VPI Board of Visitors, and a major benefactor of his alma mater.

Lights: Yes. **Seating capacity:** 52,000. **Location:** On campus. **Playing surface:** Grass. **Special features:** Locker rooms, press box, and campus book stores. **Other uses:** Commencement exercises, occasional concerts.

Original construction: 1964, at a cost of $3.5 million. Method of financing this cost was not reported. **Additions and renovations:** In 1980 12,500 seats were added to the east side stands. The north end zone was enlarged with the addition of 2,072 seats in 1999. Cost of the latter addition was $3.2 million, with private donations the source of funding. **Projected additions:** Plans are to enclose the sound end zone in 2002. In 2003 the four-level press box will be completely renovated and 10–12,000 seats will be added. That same year 1,100 club seats will be added and 52 luxury suites will be constructed. Private donations will finance the estimated cost of $44 million for these improvements.

Team name: Hokies. **Team mascot:** Hokie Bird (costumed figure). **Colors:** Maroon and orange. **Song:** "Tech Triumph." **Conference:** Big East. **First intercollegiate football game:** 1892.

Coaches and their tenure: Jerry Claiborne (1965–70), Charlie Coffey (1971–73), Jimmy Sharpe (1974–77), Bill Dooley (1978–86), Frank Beamer (1987–).

Athletic directors and their tenure: Frank Moseley (1965–77), Bill Dooley (1978–86), Dutch Baughman (1987), Dave Braine (1988–96), Jim Weaver (1997–).

Hokie Bird

WAKE FOREST UNIVERSITY
Winston-Salem, North Carolina

Groves Stadium (1968)

Named for the Groves family, major benefactors of the University. Henry Groves, one member of this family, was a Wake Forest alumnus.

Lights: Yes. **Seating capacity:** 31,500. **Location:** Off campus. **Playing surface:** Natural grass. **Special features:** Four-level press box with President's box on one level, box seats, and state-of-the-art scoreboard. **Other uses:** Each May the Crosby Clambake, held in connection with the nearby Crosby golf tournament, is held here.

Original construction: 1968, at a cost of $4 million. Private donations financed cost of construction. **Additions and renovations:** The Bridger Field House was built in 1996–97. This structure houses Athletic Department offices, Deacon Club offices, a sports lounge, Wake Forest University Hall of Fame, a locker room, and sports medicine unit. Cost of this Field House was $8 million. A fund-raising campaign and private donations financed this cost.

Team name: Demon Deacons. **Team mascot:** Demon Deacon or The Deacon (costumed figure with black top hat and tails). **Colors:** Old gold and black. **Song:** "O Here's to Wake Forest." **Conference:** Atlantic Coast. **First intercollegiate football game:** 1888.

Coaches and their tenure: Bill Tate (1968), Cal Stoll (1969–71), Tom Harper (1972), Chuck Mills (1973–78), John Mackovic (1979–80), Al Groh (1981–86), Bill Dooley (1987–92), Jim Caldwell (1993–).

Athletic directors and their tenure: Dr. Gene Hooks (1968–91), Ron Wellman (1992–).

Demon Deacon

UNIVERSITY OF WASHINGTON
Seattle, Washington

Husky Stadium (1920)

Lights: No. **Seating capacity:** 72,500. **Location:** On campus. **Playing surface:** Astroturf. **Special features:** Locker rooms, two-level press box seating 75 news media members, and elevator. The Don James Center, which can host major banquets and social events, serves as an entertainment center on game days. Nestled high above Union Bay in Lake Washington, this stadium has been voted the most scenic football venue in the nation. The north upper deck offers views of Mt. Rainier and the Olympic Mountain Range. **Other uses:** In 1990 the stadium hosted the opening and closing ceremonies as well as the track and field competition for the Goodwill Games.

Original construction: 1920, at a cost of $600,000. Method of financing this cost was not reported. **Additions and renovations:** In 1936 10,000 seats were erected around the rim of the stadium. An additional 3,000 seats were added to the north rim in 1968, the same year that Astroturf was laid on the playing field at a cost of $300,000. In 1950 15,000 seats were added on the south side at a cost of $1.7 million. The seating capacity was expanded to its current figure in 1987. Two years later the west stands were replaced to provide better seating, more concession stands and rest rooms, a police security area, and a photo deck. These improvements cost $3.7 million; the method of financing this cost was not reported. In 1989 an eight-lane synthetic surface track was installed. This cost was financed by a $1.5 million gift from the Seattle Organizing Committee for the 1990 Goodwill Games.

Team name: Huskies. **Team mascot:** Whitepaw's Arlut Spirit of Golddust (a live Alaskan malamute). **Colors:** Purple and gold. **Song:** "Bow Down to Washington." **Conference:** Pac-10. **First intercollegiate football game:** 1889.

Coaches and their tenure: Enoch Bagshew (1921–29), James Phelan (1930–41), Ralph Welch (1942–47), Howard Odell (1948–52), John Cherberg (1953–55), Darrell Royal (1956), Jim Owens (1957–74), Don James (1975–92), Jim Lambright (1993–98), Rick Neuheisel (1999–).

Athletic directors and their tenure: Darwin Meisnest (1920–27), Earl F. Campbell (1928–32), Charles Frankland (1933–35), Ray L. Eckman (1936–42), Carl V. Kilgore (1943), Alvin M. Ubrickson (1944–45), Harvey Cassill (1946–56), George Briggs (1957–59), Jim Owens (1960–68), Joe Kearney (1969–75), Mike Lude (1976–90), Barbara Hedges (1991–).

Whitepaw

WASHINGTON STATE UNIVERSITY
Pullman, Washington

Clarence D. Martin Stadium (1936)

Named in honor of Clarence D. Martin, governor of Washington during the period 1933–40, whose son Dan and daughter-in-law Charlotte donated $250,000 toward rebuilding the stadium in the 1970s.

Lights: Yes. *Seating capacity:* 37,600. *Location:* On campus. *Playing surface:* Omni-Turf. *Special features of stadium:* Press box and electronic scoreboard. Stadium is adjacent to complex housing athletic offices and locker rooms. *Other uses:* Intramural games and physical education classes.

Original construction: 1936, cost not reported. *Additions and renovation:* In 1970 south stands were rebuilt to replace stands destroyed by fire. Five years later new student stands were erected. In 1979 stadium capacity was enlarged with the addition of 12,400 seats. Cost of this addition was not reported; it was financed by private donations, the Martin family gift, gifts-in-kind, and purchase of "stadium builder" seat options. An Omni-Turf playing surface was installed in 1990. Neither the cost nor method of financing it was reported.

Team name: Cougars. *Team mascot:* Cougar (costumed figure). *Colors:* Crimson and gray. *Song:* "Cougar Fight Song." *Conference:* Pacific-10. *First intercollegiate football game:* 1894.

Coaches and their tenure: O.E. Hollingbery (1936–42), Phil Sarboe (1945–49), Forest Evashevski (1950–51), Al Kircher (1952–55), Jim Sutherland (1956–63), Bert Clark (1964–67), Jim Sweeney (1968–75), Jackie Sherrill (1976), Warren Powers (1977), Jim Walden (1978–86), Dennis Erickson (1987–88), Mike Price (1989–).

Athletic directors and their tenure: Fred Bohler (1936–49), Robert Brumblay (1950–51), Golden Romney (1952–54), Stan Bates (1955–71), Ray Nagel (1972–76), Sam Jankovich (1977–83), Dick Young (1984–87), Jim Livengood (1988–94), Rick Dickson (1995–).

Butch the Cougar

WEST VIRGINIA UNIVERSITY
Morgantown, West Virginia

Mountaineer Field (1980)

Lights: Yes. *Seating capacity:* 63,500. *Location:* On campus. *Playing surface:* Astroturf 12. *Special features:* Locker rooms, coaches' offices, luxury suites, seating for 150 news media representatives in press box, and handicapped seating in designated areas. *Other uses:* None.

Original construction: 1980, at a cost of $22 million. Cost was financed by a bond issue. *Additions and renovations:* In 1985 7,500 seats were added, with another 6,000 seats added the following year. Twelve luxury suites were constructed in 1994 and a computerized scoreboard with quad color was installed in 1995. In 1998 an indoor practice facility was completed. Cost of these improvements was $15 million; revenue earned from playing in several bowl games financed this cost.

Team name: Mountaineers. *Team mascot:* Mountaineer (costumed figure). *Colors:* Gold and blue. *Song:* "Hail, West Virginia." *Conference:* Big East. *First intercollegiate football game:* 1891.

Coaches and their tenure: Don Nehlen (1980–).

Athletic directors and their tenure: Richard Martin (1980), Fred Schaus (1981–89), Ed Pastilong (1990–).

West Virginia logo

WESTERN MICHIGAN UNIVERSITY
Kalamazoo, Michigan

Waldo Stadium (1939)

Named for Dwight B. Waldo, the first president of WMU.

Lights: Yes. *Seating capacity:* 30,200. *Location:* On campus. *Playing surface:* Prescription athletic turf. *Special features:* Locker room, weight room, training room, luxury suites that serve as coaches' offices during the week, and John Gill Stadium Club, which includes 325 chairback seats for spectators as well as press box. *Other uses:* High school football games and University soccer games.

Original construction: 1939, at a cost of $250,000. Method of financing this cost was not reported. *Additions and renovations:* Between 1939 and 1973 4,000 seats were added. In 1973 23,000 seats were added and the first artificial turf was installed. The seating capacity was expanded to the current figure in 1989. Four years later the stadium received a face-lift and prescription athletic turf was installed. In 1995 the John Gill Stadium Club was erected and a new scoreboard was installed. The Bill Brown Alumni Football Center was constructed in 1998. The center houses new coaches' offices, training room, weight room, locker room, and luxury suites. Cost of the John Gill Stadium Club was $2.6 million. The Bill Brown Center construction cost was $8 million. Both projects were financed by private donations.

Team name: Broncos. *Team mascot:* Buster Bronco (costumed figure). *Colors:* Brown and gold. *Song:* "WMU Fight Song." *Conference:* Mid-American. *First intercollegiate football game:* 1906.

Coaches and their tenure: Mike Gary (1939–41), John Gill (1942–52), Jack Petoskey (1953–56), Merle Schlosser (1957–63), Bill Doolittle (1964–74), Elliot Uzelac (1975–81), Jack Harbaugh (1982–86), Al Molde (1987–96), Gary Darnell (1997–).

Athletic directors and their tenure: Judson Hyames (1939–49), Mike Gary (1950–67), Joe Hoy (1968–79), Carl Ullrich (1980), Tom Wonderling (1981–84), Leland Byrd (1985–92), Dan Meinert (1993–95), Jim Weaver (1996–97), Kathy Beauregard (1998–).

WMU Bronco logo

UNIVERSITY OF WISCONSIN
Madison, Wisconsin

Camp Randall Stadium (1917)

The oldest stadium in the Big Ten is not named after a person but sits on a site used as a training site for Union soldiers during the Civil War, a prison for Confederate troops, and a state fairgrounds. When the Wisconsin state legislature donated the land to the University, veterans groups persuaded UW officials to name it Camp Randall to honor veterans buried in a nearby cemetery.

Lights: Yes. *Seating capacity:* 76,129. *Location:* On campus. *Playing surface:* Artificial turf. *Special features:* Locker rooms, press box, Athletic Department offices, and a display of University football memorabilia. *Other uses:* Occasional concerts, Madison Drum and Bugle Corps competitions.

Original construction: 1917, at a cost of $15,000. Method of financing this cost was not reported. *Additions and renovations:* In 1930 the Field House, formerly used to house men's and women's basketball, was built at the south end of the stadium. Bleachers were constructed against the Field House to complete its horseshoe effect. The seating capacity has been expanded several times since 1930. In 1988 the Dave McClain Athletic Facility was built adjacent to the stadium. This facility was named in memory of UW football coach Dave McClain. The 166,274 square foot structure provides a suitable environment for practice during inclement weather. The main floor features an artificial surface field (90 yards) with a ceiling high enough for kicking. The lower level contains locker rooms, training facilities, Fetzer Learning Center, and a weight room. The second level includes a theater-style auditorium with seating for 150, classrooms for individual position meetings, and a players' lounge. Construction cost of this entire facility was $9.5 million. The method of financing this cost was not reported.

Team name: Badgers. *Team mascot:* Bucky Badger (costumed figure). *Colors:* Cardinal and white. *Song:* "On, Wisconsin." *Conference:* Big Ten. *First intercollegiate football game:* 1889.

Coaches and their tenure: J.R. Richards (1917), Guy Lowman (1918), J.R. Richards (1919–22), Jack Ryan (1923–24), George Little (1925–26), Glenn Thistlethwaite (1927–31), Clarence Spears (1932–35), Harry Stuhldreher (1936–48), Ivy Williamson (1949–55), Milt Bruhn (1955–66), John Coatta (1967–69), John Jardine (1970–77), Dave McClain (1978–85), Jim Hilles (1986), Don Morton (1987–89), Barry Alvarez (1990–).

Athletic directors and their tenure: Tom E. Jones (1920–24), George Little (1925–32), Walter Meanwell (1933–35), Harry Stuhldreher (1936–50), Guy Sundt (1951–55), Ivan Williamson (1956–69), Elroy L. Hirsch (1970–87), Ade Sponberg (1988–89), Pat Richter (1990–).

UNIVERSITY OF WYOMING
Laramie, Wyoming

War Memorial Stadium (1950)

Named in honor of World War II veterans from Wyoming.

Lights: No. **Seating capacity:** 33,500. **Location:** On campus. **Playing surface:** Grass. **Special features:** Locker rooms and press box. At an elevation of 7,220 feet, War Memorial Stadium is the nation's highest football stadium. **Other uses:** Occasional summer concerts.

Original construction: 1950, at a cost of $1.5 million. State funds financed this cost. *Additions and renovations:* In 1970 5,500 seats were added. Seven years later another 8,000 seats were added, bringing capacity to its current figure. Cost of these two additions was not reported; they were financed by state funds.

Team name: Cowboys or Pokes. *Team mascot:* Cowboy Joe, a live Shetland pony. *Colors:* Brown and yellow. *Song:* "Ragtime Cowboy Joe." *Conference:* Mountain West. *First intercollegiate football game:* 1893.

Coaches and their tenure: Bowden Wyatt (1950–52), Phil Dickens (1953–56), Bob Devaney (1957–61), Lloyd Eaton (1962–70), Fritz Shurmur (1971–74), Fred Akers (1975–76), Bill Lewis (1977–79), Pat Dye (1980), Al Kincaid (1981–85), Dennis Erickson (1986), Paul Roach (1987–90), Joe Tiller (1991–96), Dana Dimel (1997–).

Athletic directors and their tenure: Glenn J. "Red" Jacoby (1950–73), George McCarty (1974–79), Bob Hitch (1980), Gary Cunningham (1981–86), Paul Roach (1987–95), Lee Moon (1996–).

Cowboy Joe IV and his Handlers

INDEX

Adams, Dave 6, 169
Adams, Emory S., Jr. 207
Agase, Alex 55, 141, 161
Aggie Memorial Stadium 60
Aillet, Joe 92
Akron, OH 6
Alabama 9, 11, 21
Albert the Alligator 59
Alborn, Ray 163
Albuquerque, NM 127
Alden, Michael 119
Alexander, William 67
Alford, Warner 115
Allen, Frank 77
Allen, Pokey 27
Allen, Terry 83
Alleva, Joe 53
Alley, Herc 111
Alley, Red 215
Allison, Stub 37
Aloha Stadium 69
Alton, Bill 191
Alumni Stadium 29
Alvarez, Barry 231
Ames, IA 79
Amodio, Paul 87
Amon G. Carter Stadium 93
Anderson, Eddie 79
Anderson, Harry 169
Anderson, Heartley "Hunk" 143
Anderson, Jerry 41
Anderson, Ladell 213
Andros, Dee 155
Ankney, Moe 31
Ann Arbor, MI 107
Annapolis, MD 209
Arbuckle, Dale 149
Archie, Mike 91
Arctic wolf 125

Arions, Bruce 185
Arizona 13, 15
Arizona Stadium 13
Arizona State University 15
Arkansas 17, 19
Arkansas State University 19
Arkeilpane, Bob 35
Armstrong, Ike 211
Arnsparger, Bill 59, 191
Arslanian, Dave 213
Arslanian, Sark 51
Athens, GA 65
Athens, OH 147
Atlanta, GA 67
Aubie 21
Auburn, AL 21
Auburn University 21
Ault, Chris 125
Austin, TX 189
Autzen Stadium 72
Avezzano, Joe 155

Babcock, George 45
Bachman, Charles 59, 109
Baddour, Richard A. 130
Bagshew, Enoch 223
Bailey, Charlie 101, 191
Baker, Art 55
Baker, Merrily D. 109
Baldacci, Paul 6
Baldwin, Dave 169
Baldwin, Jerry 179
Bale, Red 163
Ball State University 23
Ball State University Stadium 23
Bellard, Emory 117, 193
Banks, M.B. 187
Barbour, Sandy 201
Barclay, George 130

Barfield, Doug 21
Barnard, Chester 115
Barnett, Gary 49, 141
Barnhart, Mitch 155
Barnhill, John 17, 187
Barratt, Jim 155
Barrett, Ernie 85
Barry, Justin M. "Sam" 173
Bartling, Doby 215
Bartosh, Gil 191
Bartow, Gene 11
Bass, Marvin 171
Bates, Stan 225
Baton Rouge, LA 91
Battle, Bill 187
Baughman, Dutch 155, 218
Bay, Rick 113, 145, 153, 167
Baylor University 25
Beall, Bill 25
Beamer, Frank 218
Bear 25, 37
Bearcat 45
Beard, Percy 59
Bearg, Ernest E. 121
Beauregard, Kathy 229
Beaver Stadium 157
Beichly, Russ 6
Beightol, Larry 92
Belknap, Bill 73
Bell, Chuck 169, 213
Bell, Matty 193
Bell, Richard 171
Bell, Robert 31
Bellmont, L. Theo 189
Bellotti, Mike 153
Ben Hill Griffin Stadium 59
Benefiel, Chet 203
Benny Beaver 155
Berkeley, CA 37
Berndt, Jerry 163, 185
Bestwick, Dick 217

INDEX

Bible, Dana X. 121, 189, 193
Bicknell, Jack 29
Bierman, Bernie 117
Big Al 9
Big Blue 213
Bill the Goat 209
Bird, Ossian Clinton 147
Birmingham, AL 11
Bixler, Paul O. 145
Blackburn, George 45, 217
Blackledge, Ron 87
Blackman, Bob 75
Blackney, Gary 31
Blacksburg, VA 218
Blaik, Earl 207
Blake, John 149
Blaze 11
Bleymaier, Gene 27
Bloomington, IN 77
Blue Devil 53
Bobby Dodd Stadium 67
Bobcat 147
Bobinski, Michael 6
Bobo, John 19
Bockrath, Bob 9, 37, 197
Boeh, Thomas C. 147
Bohl, Allen R. 63 , 199
Bohler, Fred 225
Bohn, Mike 73
Boilermaker Special 161
Boise, ID 27
Boise State University 27
Boisture, Dan 57
Boone, J.R. 63
Boone, Pete 115
Borleske, Stan 63
Boston, McKinley 113
Boston College 29
Boulder, CO 49
Bourdet, Gene 167
Bowden, Bobby 61
Bowden, Jim 191
Bowden, Terry 21
Bowden, Tommy 47, 201
Bower, Jeff 177
Bowling Green, OH 31
Bowling Green State University 31
Bowlsby, Robert A. 79
Bowser, Charles 159
Boyd, Sam 25
Bozik, Edward J. 159
Bradley, Jim 129
Bradshaw, Jimmy 63

Braine, Dave 67, 218
Brechler, Paul 37, 79
Brennan, Terry 143
Brennan, Tom 169
Brewer, Billy 92, 115
Brewer, Chester 119
Bridgers, John 25, 61, 127
Briggs, George 223
Brigham, Bob 139
Brigham Young University 33
Britton, W.H. 187
Brodhead, Bob 91
Bronco 27, 229
Bronco Stadium 27
Bronzan, Bob 169
Brooks, Rich 153
Brothers, J.O. 203
Brown, Earl 21
Brown, Jim 185
Brown, Mack 130, 189, 201
Brown, Paul E. 145
Brown, Watson 11, 45, 163, 215
Broyles, Frank 17, 119
Bruce, Earle 51, 81, 145
Bruhn, Milt 231
Bruin 39
Brumblay, Robert 225
Brutus Buckeye 145
Bryant, Cleve 147
Bryant, Paul "Bear" 9, 193
Bryant-Denny Stadium 9
Bryne, Bill 121
Bucky Badger 231
Buffalo 49, 97
Buffalo, NY 35
Bulldog 63, 67, 92, 117
Bulldog Stadium 63
Bully 117
Burke, Brian 147
Burke, Mogan J. 161
Burnham, Elmer H. 161
Burns, Jerry 79
Burtnett, Leon 161
Busik, Bill 209
Bussey, Charles W. 92
Buster Bronco 229
Butters, Tom 53
Butts, Wally 65
Buzz 67
Byrd, Leland 229
Byrd Stadium 99
Byrne, Bill 153

Cagle, Chris 117
Cahill, Tom 207
Cain, Bill 55
Caine, John 153, 169
Caldwell, Jim 221
California 37, 39, 63, 167, 169, 173, 181
Call, William T., Jr. 207
Callahan, Ray 45
Cam the Ram 51
Cambron, Emmett F. 135
Cameron, Alan 209
Cameron, Cam 77
Cameron, Eddie 53
Camp Randall Stadium 231
Campbell, Earl F. 223
Canham, Don 107
Capka, Jerry G. 207
Cappon, Frank 83
Captain 'Cane 203
Cardinal 23, 81, 95
Carideo, Frank 119
Carillot, Vince 203
Carlen, Jim 171, 197
Carlson, Harry 49
Carmichael, W.R. 193
Carmody, Jim 177
Carr, Bill 59
Carr, Charley 117
Carr, Lloyd H. 107
Carrier Dome 183
Carson, Bud 67
Carter-Finley Stadium 133
Carver, Frank F. 159
Casale, Ernest 185
Casanova, Len 153
Casanova, Leonard J. 159
Casey, Willis 133
Cassill, Harvey 223
Casteel, Miles W. 13
Castiglione, Joe 119, 149
Cavagnaro, Charles 101, 123
Caval, Billy 171
Cavalier 217
Cavan, Mike 175
Cavanaugh, Ed 207
Cawthon, Pete 9
Cearley, Jess E. 135
Chadwick, William Dale 117
Chambers, Boyd 45
Chapel Hill, NC 130

INDEX 237

Charlottesville, VA 217
Chaump, George 209
Cherberg, John 223
Cherry, Blair 189
Chestnut Hill, MA 29
Chevigny, Jack 189
Chief Brave Spirit 137
Chief Illiniwek 75
Chief Osceola 61
Chlebek, Ed 29, 57, 87
Christiansen, Jack 181
Chui, Edward 69
Cincinnati, OH 45
Cirbus, Craig 35
Citrus Bowl 41
Clarence D. Martin Stadium 225
Clark, Bert 225
Clark, Don R. 173
Clark, Potsy 83, 121
Clausen, M.R. (Dick) 13
Clemson Memorial Stadium 47
Clemson, SC 47
Clemson University 47
Clifford B. & Audry Jones Stadium 94
Clogston, Roy B. 133
Clune, John 205
Coatta, John 231
Cobey, William 99, 130
Cochrane, Kenneth "Red" 6
Cocky 171
Cody, Josh 59
Coffey, Charlie 218
Cohen, Russ 45
Cole, George 17
Coleman, Cecil 63, 75
College Park, MD 99
College Station, TX 193
Colletto, Jim 161
Collins, Bobby 177
Collins, Chuck 130
Collins, Pat 137
Colonel Rebel 115
Colorado 49, 51, 205
Colorado Springs, CO 205
Colorado State University 51
Colson, Keith 129
Columbia, MO 119
Columbia, SC 171
Columbus, OH 145

Commonwealth Stadium 89
Conley, John 197
Connelly, Dave 199
Conover, Al 163
Cooper, John 15, 145, 203
Cooper, Ken 115
Cooper, Ron 57
Copeland, Jim 175, 211, 217
Coppedge, Bo 209
Coral Gables, FL 103
Corbett, Jim 91
Cordelli, Pete 87
Cords, Bill 191
Corrie, Bruce 141
Corrigall, Jim 87
Corrigan, Gene 143, 217
Corso, Lee 77, 139
Corvallis, OR 155
Coryell, Don 167
Cosmo the Cougar 71
Cougar 33, 71, 225
Cougar Stadium 33
Coughlin, Tom 29
Cow 35, 189
Coward, Asbury 209
Cowboy Joe 233
Cowell, R.A. 115
Cox, Ted 151
Cravath, Newell J. 173
Criner, Jim 27, 81
Crisler, Herbert O. "Fritz" 107
Crouthamel, Jake 183
Crow, John David 137, 193
Crowder, Eddie 49
Crowe, Clem 79
Crowe, Jack 17
Crowley, Jim 109
Crowton, Gary 92
Culpepper, Pat 139
Cummings, Bob 79
Cunningham, Gary A. 63, 233
Currey, Dave 45
Curry, Bill 9, 67, 89
Curtice, Jack C. 181, 211
Cutchin, Phil 151
Cutcliffe, David 115
Cy the Cardinal 81
Czekaj, Ed 157

Dale, Roland 177
Dalis, Peter 39

Dallas, TX 175
Danforth, Howard 61
Darnell, Gary 229
Darrell K. Royal Stadium 189
Dauber, Ray 117
Daugherty, Hugh "Duffy" 109
Davalos, Rudy 71, 127
Davidson, Bill 19
Davidson, Gar 207
Davie, Bob 143
Davis, Bud 49
Davis, Butch 103
Davis, Greg 201
Davis, K.E. 159
Davis, Paul 117
Davitch, Jerry 73
Dawson, Fred 121, 217
Dawson, Lowell P. "Red" 159
Dean, Joe 91
DeBerry, Fisher 205
Dee, Paul 103
DeFilippo, Gene 29
DeGroot, Dudley S. 169
Dehart, James 53
DeKalb, IL 139
Demon Deacon 221
Demoss, Bob 161
Dempsey, Cedric 13, 71
Dempsey, Rey 101
Dennison, James 6
Denton, TX 135
DePasqua, Carl A. 159
Devaney, Bob 121, 233
Devine, Don 119, 143
Devore, Hugh 143
Dickens, Phil 77, 233
Dickerson, Ron 185
Dickey, Darrell 135
Dickey, Doug 59, 187
Dickey, Jim 85
Dickson, Rick 225
Dielens, August, Jr. 207
Dienhart, Mark 113
Dietzel, Paul 77, 91, 171, 207
Diles, David 57
Dimel, Dana 233
Dix Stadium 87
Dixon, King 171
Doak S. Campbell Stadium 61

Dobbs, Bobby 191, 203
Dobbs, Glenn 203
Dockery, Rex 101, 197
Dodd, Bobby 67
Dodds, Deloss 85, 189
Doherty, Edward A. 13
Donahue, Terry 39
Doninger, Clarence 77
Donnan, Jim 65, 97
Donnelly, Boots 111
Donomedi, Herb 43
Dooley, Bill 130, 218, 221
Dooley, Vince 65
Doolittle, Bill 229
Douglas, Otis W. 6, 17
Dowd, Barry 19
Dowdy-Ficklen Stadium 55
Dowhower, Rod 181, 215
Dowler, Thomas 6
Doyt L. Perry Stadium 31
Drakulich, Chub 123
Drew, Harold "Red" 9, 115
Driver, James G. 217
Dry, F.A. 195, 203
DuBose, Mike 9
Duck 153
Dufek, Don 87
Duffner, Mark 99
Duke University 53
Dull, Richard M. 99
Duncan, Donnie 81, 149
Dunn, Clair 199
Dunn, Eddie 103
Dunn, Joe Lee 115
Durham, NC 53
Dye, Pat 21, 55, 233
Dye, "Tippy" 121, 141
Dykes, Spike 197

Eagle 29, 57, 87, 177
Earle, Jimmy 111
East Carolina University 55
East Lansing, MI 109
Eastern Michigan University 57
Eaton, Lloyd 233
Eaves, Joel 65
Eckman, Ray L. 223
Edwards, Bill 215
Edwards, Earle 133
Edwards, George 119
Edwards, LaVell 33

El Paso, TX 191
Elias, Bill 209, 217
Eliot, Ray 75
Ellender, Bennie 201
Ellington, Bill 189
Elliott, Chalmers "Bump" 79, 107
Elliott, E.C. 161
Elliott, Pete 37, 75, 103, 121
Ellis, Dick 25
Elward, A.H. Mal 161
Elway, Jack 169, 181
Emory, Ed 55
Engelhardt, Greg 37
England, Forrest 199
Engle, Rip 157
English, Wally 201
Enke, Fred A. 13
Enright, Dick 153
Enright, Rex 171
Erfurth, Augie 163
Erickson, Charles P. 130
Erickson, Dennis 73, 103, 225, 233
Ettlinger, H.J. 189
Eugene, OR 153
Evans, Clint 37
Evans, George "Chick" 139
Evanston, IL 141
Evashevski, Forest 79, 225
Everest, Andy 135
Exedine, Albert A. 151

F.C. "Phog" Allen 83
Fairbanks, Chuck 49, 149
Falcon 31, 205
Falcon Stadium 205
Fambrough, Don 83
Farwick, A.W. "Gus" 13
Fassel, Jim 211
Faulkinberry, Russ 179
Faurot, Don 119
Faust, Gerry 6, 143
Fayetteville, AR 17
Fazio, Serafino "Foge" 159
Fehlberg, Rondo 33
Feldman, Rudy 127
Felker, Rockey 117
Ferentz, Kirk 79
Ferrin, Arnie 211
Fertig, Craig 155
Ferzacca, "Frosty" 57
Fesler, Wesley E. 145, 159

Fetzer, Robert 130
Fischer, Bob 39
Fitzgerald, Dennis 87
Fletcher, Howard 139
Florida 41, 59, 61, 103
Florida State University 61
Floyd, Don 19
Floyd, Johnny "Red" 111
Floyd, Ralph 77
Floyd Casey Stadium 25
Flynn, Dick 43
Flynn, William J. 29
Foldberg, Hank 193
Foley, Jeremy N. 59
Folsom Field 49
Ford, Danny 17, 47
Ford, Tom 71
Fort Collins, CO 51
Fort Worth, TX 195
Forzana, Rick 209
Foster, Bill 141
Foster, Ralph K. 171
Fouke, Harry 71
Fouts, Thereon J. 135
Fouts Field 135
Fowler, Lee 111
Franchione, Dennis 127, 195
Francis, A.G. "Barney" 199
Frankland, Charles 223
Franks, Carl 53
Freddie Falcon 31
Frederick, Bob 83
Frei, Jerry 153
Fresno, CA 63
Fresno State University 63
Frieda Falcon 31
Frnka, Henry 203
Fry, Hayden 79, 135
Fulcher, Bill 67
Fuller, Leon 51
Fulmer, Phillip 187
Fuoss, Donald E. 111

Gainesville, FL 59
Gallagher, Ed 151
Garner, Jim 151
Garrett, Mike 173
Gary, Mike 229
Gass, Floyd 151
Geiger, Andy 99, 145, 181
George, Raymond 193

Georgia 65, 67
Georgia Institute of Technology 67
Gerald J. Ford Stadium 175
Giannini, Richard 137
Gibbs, Gary 149
Gibson, Bob 31
Gibson, Claude 203
Gibson, Vince 85, 201
Giel, Paul 113
Gilbert, Claude 167, 169
Gilbertson, Keith 37, 73
Gill, John 229
Gill, "Slats" 155
Gillman, Sid 45
Gish, H.D. 121
Gladchuck, Kevin 201
Gladchuk, Chet 71
Glass Bowl 199
Glassford, Bill 121
Gleason, Ken 63
Goff, Ray 65
Goin, Bob 45, 61
Golden eagle 87
Goldsmith, Fred 53, 163
Goldy Gopher 113
Gonzales, Al 129
Goss, Tom A. 107
Gottfried, Mike 45, 83, 159
Graber, Doug 165
Grandelius, Sonny 49
Graves, Ray 59
Green, Dennis 141, 181
Green, Leon 73
Green, Jack 215
Greenville, NC 55
Greenwood, Don 199
Gregory, Jack 31
Grese, Warren 171
Griffith, Johnny 65
Grobe, Jim 147
Groff, Wally 193
Groh, Al 221
Groth, Cary 139
Grover, Brandon T. "Butch" 147
Groves Stadium 221
Gruninger, Fred 165
Guenther, Ron 75
Guepe, Art 215, 217
Gustafson, Andy 103
Gutekunst, John 113

Hackett, Paul 173
Hagan, Cliff 89
Hagan, James 159
Hall, Dale 207
Hall, Galen 59
Hall, Skip 27
Hallman, Curley 91, 177
Hamilton, Brutis 37
Hamilton, Tom 159
Hamrick, Mike 55
Hancock, J.W. 117
Harbaugh, Jack 229
Hardage, Lewie 149
Hardin, Wayne 185, 209
Harding, Jack 103
Hardy, Leslie P. 6
Hargiss, Bill 83
Harkema, Jim 57
Harp, Tom 53
Harper, Jesse 143
Harper, Tom 221
Harper, Warren 191
Harris, Charles 15
Harris, Leo 63
Harris, Walt 159
Harrison, W. Don 159
Hart, Dave, Jr. 55, 61, 119
Hart, David R. 159
Harth, William H. 171
Hartranft, Tiny 169
Haskell, Lawrence 149
Hatfield, Ken 17, 47, 163, 205
Hattiesburg, MS 177
Hawaii 69
Hawk 195, 211
Hayes, E.C. 117
Hayes, W.W. "Woody" 145
Hazel, Homer 115
Heard, T.P. 91
Hedges, Barbara 223
Heffer, Ernie 29
Heisman, John 67
Helsel, Dennis 6
Helton, Kim 71
Helwig, Craig 135
Henderson, Bill 25
Henderson, Elmer C. 173, 203
Henning, Dan 29
Henry, Gwinn 83, 119
Henshaw, George 203
Herbie Husker 121
Herky 79

Hess, Bill 147
Hess, Jim 129
Hey Reb 115
Hickey, Jim 130
Hicks, John W. 161
Hill, Chris 211
Hill, Jesse T. "Jess" 173
Hill, Mary Alice 167
Hill, Pat 63
Hilles, Jim 231
Hilyer, Jim 11
Hindman, Hugh 145
Hirsch, Elroy L. 231
Hitch, Bob 233
Hoeppner, Terry 105
Hoffman, Randy 169
Hogan, Harold "Bo" 163
Hokie Bird 218
Holcomb, Stuart K. 141, 161
Holland, Terry 217
Hollingbery, O.E. 225
Hollis, Benny 137
Hollis, Joe 19
Holmoe, Tom 37
Holovak, Mike 29
Holtkamp, Fred 117
Holtz, Lou 17, 113, 133, 171
Honolulu, HI 69
Hooks, Gene 221
Hoolahan, Paul 215
Horton, Jeff 123, 125
Houghton, William "Bud" 6
Houston, TX 71, 163
Hovious, Brad 19, 91
Howard, Frank 47
Howard, Wayne 211
Hubbard, Bill 169
Hubert H. Humphrey Metrodome 52
Hudspeth, Tommy 191
Hughes Stadium 51
Hunt, Joel 65
Hunter, Gary 73
Hunter, Willis O. 173
Huntington, WV 97
Hurf, George 75
Hurt, Ben 111
Hurt, Vic 203
Huskie Stadium 139
Husky Stadium 223
Hyames, Judson 229

Hyde, Harvey 123
Hyman, Eric 105, 195

Iba, Henry P. 151
Idaho 27, 73
Illinois 75, 139, 141
Indian family 19
Indian Stadium 19
Indiana 23, 77, 143, 161
Indiana University 77
Ingram, Bill 37
Ingram, Hootie 9, 47, 61
Ingwersen, Burg 79
Iowa 79, 81
Iowa City, IA 79
Iowa State University 81
Ippoliti, Jerry 139
Ireland, Bill 123
Irvin, Barlow 193
Isbell, Cecil 161

Jack, James R. "Bud" 211
Jack Trice Stadium 81
Jacoby, Glenn J. "Red" 233
James, Carl 53, 99
James, Don 87, 223
Jankovich, Sam 103, 225
Jardine, John 231
Jayhawk 83
Jaymes, Oval 51
Jaynes, L. Oval 159
Jenike, Bill 45
Jenkins, John 71
Jennings, Bill 121
Jennings, Morley 197
Jensen, Clayne 33
Jermier, John "Jersey" 85
Joe Aillet Stadium 92
Joe Vandal 73
Johnson, Corey 51
Johnson, Jimmy 103, 151
Johnson, Monte 83
Johnson, R.C. 101, 105, 185
Jones, Arthur 63
Jones, Don 41
Jones, Edgar Charles 59
Jones, Gomer 149
Jones, Howard H. 173
Jones, Jim 145
Jones, June 69
Jones, Larry 61
Jones, Lawrence 91, 121, 149, 207
Jones, Pat 151

Jones, T. 197
Jones, Tom E. 231
Jordan, Ralph 21
Jordan-Hare Stadium 21
Jurich, Tom 51, 95

Kalamazoo, MI 229
Kansas 83, 85
Kansas Memorial Stadium 83
Kansas State University 85
Kapp, Joe 37
Kappes, Bob 147
Karr, Ken 55
Karr, O. Ken, Jr. 167
Kasser, John 37, 71
Kearney, Joe 223
Kearney, Joseph 109
Keasler, Bobby 137
Keene, R.S. "Spec" 155
Kehoe, James 99
Keilitz, Dave 43
Kellogg, N.A. 161
Kelly-Shorts Stadium 43
Kenan Memorial Stadium 130
Kennedy, Laing 87
Kent, OH 87
Kent State University 87
Kentucky 89, 95
Kerr, Andrew 181
Kibbie Dome 73
Kichefski, Walt 103
Kiffin, Monte 133
Kilgore, Carl V. 223
Kinard, Billy R. 115
Kincaid, Al 19
Kincaid, Pat 233
Kines, Joe 17
King, Dana 45
King, Dewey 169
King, George S., Jr. 161
King, J.T. 197
Kinnick Stadium 79
Kipke, Harry G. 107
Kircher, Al 225
Kizer, Noble E. 161
Kjolhede, Ted 43
Klooz, Karl 83
Knap, Tony 27, 123
Knightro 41
Knoll, Mike 129
Knoxville, TN 187
Koenig, John 127

Koetter, Dirk 27
Kragthorpe, Dave 155, 213
Kramer, Roy 43, 215
Krause, Edward "Moose" 143
Krivak, Joe 99
Kruczek, Mike 41
Krueger, Gil 129
Krueger, Phil 63, 213
KSU Stadium 85
Kuharich, Joe 143
Kush, Frank 15
Kyle Field 193

Lacewell, Larry 19
Lafayette, LA 85
Lahar, Harold 71
Lambright, Jim 223
Lambright, Maxie 92
Lancaster, Harry 89
Landreth, Orlan M. 13
Lane Stadium 218
Laramie, WY 233
Larche, Harry 199
Larkins, Dick 145
Larson, Gordon K. 6
LaRue, Jim 13
Las Cruces, NM 129
Las Vegas, NV 123
Lauer, Edward 79
Lauterbur, Frank X. 79, 199
Lawlor, Jake 125
Lawrence, Don 217
Lawrence, KS 83
Layden, Elmer 143
Leahy, Frank 143
Lee, Clyde 71
Lee, David 191
Legion Field 11
Leland, Ted 181
Lengyel, Jack 63, 119, 209
Leprechaun 143
Lessig, James 31, 83
Lester, Roy 99
Levy, Marv 37
Lewandowski, Adolph J. 121
Lewis, Bill 55, 67, 233
Lewis Field 71
Lexington, KY 89
Liberty Bowl Mem. Stadium 101
Lichtenberg, Tom 147

INDEX

Lieb, Tom 59
Lightning 111
Lil Red 121
Lincoln, NE 121
Lindsey, Add 83
Lindsey, Adrian 149
Liske, Pete 73, 199
Little, George 231
Littlefield, Clyde 189
Livengood, Jim 13, 225
Lobo Louie 127
Logan, Steve 55
Logan, UT 213
Lonborg, Arthur "Dutch" 83
Long, James W. 199
Long, Rocky 127
Longhorn steer 189
Lookabaugh, Jim 151
Los Angeles, CA 39, 173
Los Angeles Memorial Stadium 82
Louisiana 91, 92, 137, 179, 201
Louisiana State University 91
Louisiana Tech University 92
Louisiana Superdome 201
Louisville, KY 95
Louthern, Ray 23
Lovat, Tom 211
Lowman, Guy 231
Lubbock, TX 197
Lubick, Sonny 51
Lude, Mike 21, 51, 87, 223
Luginbill, Al 167
Luster, Dewey "Snorter" 149
Lynch, Bill 23

M.M. Roberts Stadium 177
MacIntyre, George 215
Mackay Stadium 125
MacKenzie, Jim 149
Mackey, Guy J. 161
Mackovic, John 75, 189, 221
MacLeod, Judy 203
MacPherson, Dick 183
Maddox, Carl 91, 117
Madigan, Slip 79
Madison, WI 231
Maggard, Dave 37, 103

Majors, John 159, 187
Mallios, Harry 103
Mallory, Bill 49, 77, 139
Malone Stadium 64, 137
Maloney, Frank 183
Manhattan, KS 85
Mans, George 57
Marche, Vaughn 61
Marco 97
Marcum, Bob 83, 171
Mariucco, Steve 37
Marmie, Larry 15
Marolt, Bill 49
Marshall University 97
Marshall University Stadium 97
Martin, Abe 195
Martin, Ben 205, 217
Martin, Maurice 205
Martin, Richard 227
Maryland 99, 209
Mason, Glen 83, 87, 113
Mason, Tony 13, 45
Massachusetts 29
Masters, Al 181
Masterton, Bernie 121
Mather, Chuck 83
Maturi, Joel 105
Maulbetsch, John F. 151
May, Bobby 163
McBride, Ron 211
McCain, Fred 135
McCallister, Don 171
McCarney, Dan 81
McCartney, Bill 49
McCarty, George 191, 233
McClain, Dave 23, 111
McClellan, Bill 47
McCollum, Andy 111
McCoy, Ernest 157
McCoy, Ernie 103, 157
McCullough, Lou 81
McDavid, Pete 127
McDonald, H.C. 169
McDonald, Jim 187
McDonald, Lavon 127
McDonald, Ned 217
McDowell, Gene 41
McDuffie, Richard 135
McElhaney, Harold 147
McEver, Gene 130
McEwan, John 207
McGee, Mike 45, 53, 55, 171, 173

McGraw, Thurman "Fum" 51
McGugin, Dan 215
McKale, J.F. "Pop" 13
McKay, John 173
McKechnie, Ross 117
McKeen, Allyn 117
McKeever, Ed 143
McLaren, George 45
McLellan, Bill 177
McLendon, Charlie 91
McMillan, Johnnie 171
McMullen, Joseph 6, 169
McWilliams, David 189, 197
Meagher, Jack 21
Meanwell, Walter 231
Meek, Bill 71, 211
Mehre, Harry 65, 115
Meinert, Dan 229
Meisnest, Darwin 223
Mellard, Jim 139
Memorial Stadium (CA) 37
Memorial Stadium (IL) 75
Memorial Stadium (IN) 77
Memorial Stadium (NE) 121
Memorial Stadium/Faurot Field 119
Memphis, TN 101
Menefee, Bill 25
Merritt, Frank 205
Metzenthin, W.E. 189
Meyer, Carl 45
Meyer, Dutch 195
Meyer, Joe 45
Meyer, Ron 123
Meyers, Jim 193
Miami University (Ohio) 105
Michael, Bill 191
Michaels, Al 133
Michelosen, John P. 159
Michie Stadium 99
Michigan 57, 107, 109, 229
Michigan Stadium 107
Michigan State University 109
Middle Tennessee State University 111
Midgett, E.W. 111
Milehan, Charles 45

Miller, Charles 121
Miller, Fred 15, 167
Miller, Jim 29
Miller, Paul 92
Miller, Steve 85
Milligan, Walter S. 159
Mills, Chuck 213, 221
Mills, Douglas 75
Minneapolis, MN 113
Minnesota 113
Minter, Rick 45
Mississippi 115, 117, 177
Mississippi State, MS 117
Mississippi State University 117
Missouri 119
Mr. and Mrs. Wuf 133
Mr. Commodore 215
Mitchell, Jack 17, 83
Mitchell, Odus 135
Moeller, Gary 75, 107
Molde, Al 229
Mollenkopf, Jack 161
Monahan, W.W. "Bill" 37
Mondt, Bill 127
Monroe, LA 137
Mont, Tommy 99
Moon, Lee 97, 233
Moore, Bernie 91
Moore, Bud 83
Moore, Jerry 135, 197
Moore, Perry 51
Moos, Bill 153
Moran, J.P. 171
Morgan, Dell 197
Morgantown, WV 227
Morrison, Joe 127, 171
Morrison, Ray 215
Morton, Don 203, 231
Morton, Jack 199
Morton, Slick 117
Moscow, ID 73
Moseley, Frank 218
Moss, Perry 61
Mount Pleasant, MI 43
Mountaineer 227
Mountaineer Field 227
Mudra, Darrell 13, 61
Mulcahy, Bob 165
Mule 207
Mullally, Mike 27
Mumme, Hal 89
Muncie, IN 23

Munn, Clarence "Biggie" 109
Murfreesboro, TN 111
Murphy, Billy J. 101
Murphy, Bob 169
Murphy, Charles M. 111
Murphy, Jack 199
Murphy, Raymond 207
Murphy, Tim 45
Murray, Bill 53
Murray, Frank 217
Myers, Gerald 197
Myers, Wave 23
Myslinski, Casimir J. 159

Nagel, Ray 69, 79, 211, 225
Nashville, TN 215
Navy-Marine Corps Memorial Stadium 100
Nebraska 121
Neely, Jess 163, 215
Negratti, Al 123
Nehlen, Don 31, 227
Nelson, "Corky" 135
Nelson, Spike 117
Ness, Gary 127
Neuheisel, Rick 49, 223
Nevada 123, 125
New Brunswick, NJ 165
New Jersey 165
New Mexico 127, 129
New Mexico State University 129
New Orleans, LA 201
New York 35, 183, 207
Newell, Pete 37
Newton, C.M. 89
Newton, William 171
Neyland, R.R. 187
Neyland Stadium 187
Nichols, Luther A. 37
Nippert Stadium 45
Nittany Lion 157
Noble, C.R. "Dudy" 115, 117
Nolting, Ray 45
Norman, OK 149
North Carolina 53, 55, 130, 133, 221
North Carolina State University 133
Northeast Louisiana University 137
Northern Illinois University 139

Northwestern University 141
Norton, Homer 193
Norvell, Merritt J. 109
Notre Dame, IN 143
Notre Dame Stadium 143
Novak, Joe 139
Nugent, Tom 61, 99
Nunnely, Wayne 123
Nutt, Houston 17, 27

Oakes, Bunnie 49
Oakes, Jim 92
O'Brien, Dave 185
O'Brien, Tom 29
O'Cain, Mike 133
O'Dell, Gerald 45, 139
Odell, Howard 223
Oestrike, Ron 57
Ohio 6, 31, 45, 87, 105, 145, 147, 199
Ohio Stadium 145
Ohio State University 145
Ohio University 147
Oklahoma 149, 151, 203
Oklahoma Memorial Stadium 149
Oklahoma State University 151
O'Leary, George 67
O'Leary, Jack 41, 51
Oliver, G.A. "Tex" 13
Olle, Ed 189
Olsen, Al 167
Onofrio, Al 119
Oosterbaan, Bennie G. 107
Orange Bowl Stadium 103
Oregon 153, 155
Oregon State University 155
Orlando, FL 41
Orwig, Bill 77, 199
Orwig, J.W. 121
Osborne, Tom 121
Otto the Orange 183
Oval, Jaymes 73
Owen, Bennie 149
Owens, Jim 223
Owens, Lee 6
Owens, Steve 149
Owl 163, 185
Oxford, MS 115
Oxford, OH 105

INDEX

Pace, Bill 215
Padilla, Bob 63
Pancoast, Fred 101, 215
Panther 159
Papa John's Cardinal Stadium 95
Parcells, Bill 205
Pardee, Jack 71
Parker, Dennis 135
Parker, Paul B. 117, 187
Parker, Red 47
Parker Stadium 155
Parrish, Stan 85
Parseghian, Ara 141, 143
Pasqualoni, Paul 183
Pastilong, Ed 227
Paterno, Joe 157
Patterson, Bob 101
Patterson, Jack 25
Patterson, Pat 92
Paul, Jim 129
Paydirt Pete 191
Payseur, Thodore B. 141
Peace, Joe Raymond 92
Pearson, Alvin 63
Peay, Francis 141
Peck, Bill 111
Peden, Don 147
Peden Stadium 147
Pederson, Steve 159
Pees, Dean 87
Pell, Charley 47, 59
Pella, Chris 213
Pennsylvania 157, 159, 185
Pennsylvania State University 157
Perkins, Lew 99
Perkins, Ray 9, 19
Perles, George 109
Perry, Doyt 31
Perry, Richard 173
Peruna 175
Peterson, Bill 41, 61, 263
Petoskey, Jack 229
Pettibone, Jerry 139, 155
Phelan, James M. 161, 223
Philadelphia, PA 185
Phillips, Terry Don 151
Pinkel, Gary 199
Pirate 55
Pistol Pete 129, 151
Pitt Stadium 159
Pittman, Jim 195
Pittsburgh, PA 159

Pixlee, James E. 151
Pont, John 77, 141
Potts, Frank 49
Powers, Warren 119, 225
Presnell, Glenn 121
Price, Edwin Booth 189
Price, Larry 69
Price, Mike 225
Price, Nibs 37
Priestly, Kenneth 37
Primmer, Bob 23
Pritchett, Norton 217
Prothro, Tommy 155
Provo, UT 33
Pruett, Bob 97
Pryor, Dean 19
Puddington, Dave 87
Pullman, WA 225
Purdue University 161
Purvis, Don 9

Qualcomm Stadium 167
Quigley, E.C. 83

Rabenhorst, Harry 91
Rader, David 203
Rafalko, Edmund 205
Raider Red 197
Rainbow warrior 69
Rainsberger, Ellis 85
Raleigh, NC 133
Ralphie IV 49
Ralston, John 169, 181
Ram 51, 130
Rameses 130
Randle, Sonny 55, 217
Rasnick, Rick 57
Razorback 17
Razorback Stadium 17
Read, Don 153
Reed, Tom 133
Reedy, Chuck 25
Rein, Bo 133
Renegade 61
Reno, NV 125
Reveille VI 193
Rice, Homer 45, 67, 130, 163
Rice Stadium 163
Rice University 163
Rice-Eccles Stadium 211
Richards, J.R. 231
Richards, Milt 85
Richter, Pat 231

Riley, Mike
Riptide 201
Ritchey, Norv 153
Roach, Paul 233
Robbins, Fred 115
Roberson, Joe 107
Roberts, Dave 25, 137
Robertson, Sam 179
Robertson Stadium 71
Robinson, Bobby 47
Robinson, Harvey 187
Robinson, John 123, 173
Robinson, Les 133
Robinson, Sid 117
Robison, Polk 197
Rockne, Knute 143
Rocky the Rocket 199
Roderick, Myron 151
Rodgers, Pepper 67, 83
Rogers, Darryl 15, 63, 109, 169
Rohr, William D. 147
Romney, Golden 225
Rose, Glen 17
Rose, Tim 105
Rose Bowl 39
Rosenthal, Dick 143
Ross, Bobby 67, 99
Ross-Ade Stadium 161
Rothermel, Brad 123
Rubber Bowl 6
Ruetz, Joe 181
Rush, Clive 199
Rust, Rod 135
Ruston, LA 92
Rutgers Stadium 165
Rutgers University 165
Ryan, Jack 231
Ryan Field 141
Rynearson Stadium 57

Saban, Lou 41, 99, 103, 109, 141
Sadler, Charlie 139
St. John, Lynn 145
Saira, Charley 117
Salem, Joe 113
Salt Lake City, UT 211
Sam Boyd Stadium 123
Sammy the Owl 163
Samuel, Tony 129
San Diego, CA 167
San Diego State University 167

243

INDEX

San Jose, CA 169
San Jose State University 169
Sanders, Red 215
Sanford Stadium 65
Sarboe, Phil
Sarklon, Frank 15
Sasse, Ralph 117, 207
Sauer, George 25, 83
Saunders, William 49
Scarlet Knight 165
Scattini, Jerry 125
Scelfo, Chris 201
Scesniak, Dick 87
Schaus, Fred 227
Schembechler, Glenn E. 107
Scherer, Rip 101
Schexnayder, Nelson 179
Schlosser, Merle 229
Schmidt, Francis A. 145, 195
Schnellenberger, Howard 103, 149
Schroeder, Ernest G. 79
Schudel, Paul 9
Schuder, William J. 207
Schultz, Dick 217
Schwartz, Marchmont 181
Schweitzer, Kenny 205
Scott, Brad 171
Scott, Charley 117
Scott Field 117
Scott Stadium 217
Scovil, Doug 167
Scrappy 135
Seattle, WA 223
Sebastian the Ibis 103
Sebo, Steve 217
Seger, Andrea 23
Selmer, Carl 103
Setencich, Lyle 27
Seymour 177
Shafer, John 115
Shank, Henry 83
Sharp, Charley 117
Sharpe, Jimmy 218
Shaughnessy, Clark D. 159, 181
Shaw, Buck 37
Shea, Terry 165, 169
Sheehan, Mel 119
Shelton, Chuck 213
Sheppard, Mike 127

Sheridan, Dick 133
Sheriff, Stan 69
Sherrill, Jackie 117, 159, 193, 225
Shofner, Jim 195
Shoults, Paul 57
Shrider, Richard 105
Shurmur, Fritz 233
Sikes, J.V. 83
Simmons, Bob 151
Simon, Matt 135
Simpson, Chauncey 119
Simrell, Dan 199
Single, Doug 141
Skelly Stadium 203
Sloan, Russ 63
Sloan, Steve 9, 41, 115, 135, 197
Slocum, R.C. 193
Smith, Albert 57
Smith, Andy 37
Smith, Clyde B. 15
Smith, Dave 151
Smith, Eugene 57
Smith, George 45
Smith, Homer 207
Smith, J. Burt 109
Smith, John L. 73, 95, 213
Smith, Larry 13, 119, 173, 201
Smith, Lyle 27
Smith, Tad 115
Smith, Vern 199
Smokey 187
Snavely, Carl 130
Snyder, Bill 85
Snyder, Bruce 15, 37, 213
Snyder, Lynn 155
Snyder, Robert 199
Solem, Ossie 79
Solich, Frank 121
Sooner Schooner 149
Soshink, Joseph 121
South Carolina 47, 171
Southern Methodist University 175
Spartan 169
Spartan Stadium 109, 169
Sparty 109
Spears, Clarence "Doc" 199, 231
Speegle, Cliff 151
Spetman, Randall 205
Sponberg, Ade 231

Spurrier, Steve 53, 59
Stahley, J.N. 199
Stalcup, Wilbur 119
Stallings, Gene 9
Stanford, CA 181
Stanford, John 111
Stanford Stadium 181
Stanford University 181
Stanley, D.K. "Dutch" 59
Stanley, Jim 151
Stanton, Tom 25
Stapleton, Clay 61, 215
Stasavich, Clarence 55
State University, AR 19
State University of New York at Buffalo 35
Staub, Ralph 45
Steele, Kevin 25
Stegeman, Herman J. 65
Stewart, E.J. "Doc" 189
Stidham, Tom 149
Stiles, Lynn 169
Stillwater, OK 151
Stinson, Wade R. 83
Stiteler, Harry 193
Stobart, Chuck 101, 199, 211
Stock, Mike 57
Stokley, Nelson 179
Stoll, Cal 221
Stolz, Denny 31, 109, 167
Stoner, Neale 75
Stoops, Bob 149
Stovall, Jerry 91, 92
Strack, David 13
Strong, Jim 123
Stuhldreher, Harry 231
Stull, Bob 119, 191
Sullivan, Pat 195
Sullivan, R.L. 115
Sun Bowl 191
Sun Devil 15
Sun Devil Stadium 15
Sundt, Guy 231
Sunseri, Sal 159
Super Frog 195
Sutherland, Jim 225
Sutherland, John B. "Jock" 159
Sutton, Bob 207
Sweeney, Jim 63, 225
Switzer, Barry 149
Swofford, John 130
Swoop 105, 211

INDEX 245

Syracuse, NY 183
Syracuse University 183

Tallahassee, FL 61
Tamburo, Dick 15, 197
Tammariello, Augie 179
Tarman, Jim 157
Tate, Bill 221
Tate, Charlie 103
Tate, Marvin 193
Tatum, Jim 99, 130, 149
Taylor, Charles A. 181
Taylor, Fred 195
Taylor, Kip 155
Taylor, Rick 45, 141
Teaff, Grant 25
Tebell, Gus 217
Teevens, Buddy 201
Tempe, AZ 15
Temple University 185
Templeton, Larry 117
Tennessee 101, 111, 187, 215
Tepper, Lou 75
Testudo the Terrapin 99
Texas 25, 71, 135, 163, 175, 189, 191, 193, 195, 197
Texas A&M University 193
Texas Christian University 195
Texas Tech University 197
Tharp, Dick 49
Theder, Roger 37
Theokas, Charlie 185
Thistlethwaite, Glenn 231
Thomas, Frank 9
Thompson, John 191
Thomsen, Fred 17
Thornhill, C.E. 181
Thornton, Charley 19
Tiger 21, 47, 91, 101, 119
Tiger Stadium 91
Tiller, Joe 161, 233
Tinsley, Gaynell 91
Tisdel, Jeff 125
Titchenal, Bob 169
Toeller, Rod 213
Tohill, Billy 195
Toledo, Bob 39
Toledo, OH 199
Tollner, Ted 167, 173
Tom II 101
Tomburo, Dick 119
Tomey, Dick 13, 69
Tomlin, John 17

Torbush, Carl 92, 130
Tormey, Chris 73
Towers, Dick 85
Townsend, Nelson 35
Trachok, Dick 125
Tranquill, Gary 209
Traveler 173
Travis, Larry 85
Troxel, Ed 73
Truman the Tiger 119
Tubbs, Irl 79
Tuberville, Tommy 21, 115
Tuckett, Glen 33
Tucson, AZ 13
Tulane University 201
Tulsa, OK 203
Turner, Ron 75, 169
Turner, Todd 133, 215
Tuscaloosa, AL 9
Tyler, Bob 117, 135

UGA V (bulldog) 65
Ubrickson, Alvin M. 223
Ullrich, Carl 207, 229
Underwood, Clarence 109
University of Akron 6
University of Alabama–Birmingham 11
University of Alabama–Tuscaloosa 9
University of Arizona 13
University of Arkansas 17
University of California–Berkeley 37
University of California–Los Angeles 39
University of Central Florida 41
University of Cincinnati 45
University of Colorado 49
University of Florida 59
University of Georgia 65
University of Hawaii 69
University of Houston 71
University of Idaho 73
University of Illinois 75
University of Iowa 79
University of Kansas 83
University of Kentucky 89
University of Louisville 95
University of Maryland 99
University of Memphis 101
University of Miami 103

University of Michigan 107
University of Minnesota 113
University of Mississippi 115
University of Missouri 119
University of Nebraska 121
University of Nevada–Las Vegas 123
University of Nevada–Reno 125
University of New Mexico 127
University of North Carolina 130
University of North Texas 135
University of Oklahoma 149
University of Oregon 153
University of Pittsburgh 159
University of South Carolina 171
University of Southern California 173
University of Southern Mississippi 177
University of Southwestern Louisiana 179
University of Tennessee 187
University of Texas–Austin 189
University of Texas–El Paso 191
University of Toledo 199
University of Tulsa 203
University of Utah 211
University of Virginia 217
University of Washington 223
University of Wisconsin 231
University of Wyoming 233
University of Notre Dame 143
University Park, PA 157
University Stadium 127
Urbana-Champaign, IL 75
Urich, Richard 139
Urick, Max 81, 85

246 INDEX

U.S. Air Force Academy 205
U.S. Military Academy 207
U.S. Naval Academy 209
Utah 33, 211, 213
Utah State University 213
Uzelac, Elliot 209, 229

Valek, Jim 75
Valesente, Bob 83
Valvano, Jim 133
Vanatta, Bob 92
Vance, Gene 75
Vanderbilt Stadium 215
Vanderbilt University 215
Vanderbush, Al 207
Vanderlinden, Ron 99
Van De Velde, Bruce 213
Van Galder, Clark 63
Van Gent, C.E. 181
Vaught, John H. 115
Vaught-Hemingway Stadium 115
Vellen, Don 61
Ventura, Rick 141
Veterans Stadium 185
Virginia 217, 218
Virginia Polytechnic Institute and State University 218
Voigts, Bob 141
von Appen, Fred 69
Voris, Richard 217
Voyles, Carl 21

Wacker, Jim 113, 195
Waco, TX 25
Wade, Wallace 9, 53
Wadsworth, Mike 143
Wagner, Bob 69
Wake Forest University 221
Walden, Jim 81, 225
Waldo Stadium 229
Waldorf, Lynn 37, 141, 151
Walker, Clyde 83
Walker, Ed L. 115
Walker, Randy 105, 141
Walker, Wade 117, 149
Wall, Hindman 45, 201
Wallace, Bobby 185
Wallace, Dwight 23
Wallace, Jewell 71
Wallace Wade Stadium 53

Waller, E.M. 111
Walsh, Bill 181
Wampfler, Jerry 51
War Memorial Stadium 233
Ward, Bob 99
Ward, Dallas 49
Ward, Jim 35
Warmath, Murray 117
Warner, Glenn "Pop" 181
Washington 223, 225
Washington State University 225
Watters, Frank "Muddy" 109
Weatherbie, Charlie 209, 213
Weaver, Dewitt 197
Weaver, Douglas 67, 109
Weaver, Ed 145
Weaver, Jim 123, 218, 229
Weber, Robert W. 13
Weeks, Bill 127
Weidenbach, Jack 107
Weir, Sam 41
Weiser, Tim 51, 57
Welch, Ralph 223
Wellman, Ron 221
Welsh, George 209, 217
West, Lance 97
West, Tommy 47
West Lafayette, IN 76
West Point, NY 207
West Virginia 97, 227
West Virginia University 227
Western Michigan University 229
White, Gavin 185
White, Kevin 15, 201
White, Mike 37, 75
Whitworth, J.B. 9, 151
Widdoes, Carroll C. 145, 147
Widenhofer, Woody 119, 215
Wieman, Elton E. "Tad" 107
Wiggin, Paul 181
Wilce, John W. 145
Wildcat 13, 83, 85
Wilkinson, Bud 149
Willaman, Sam S. 145
Williams, A.L. 92
Williams, Dan 153

Williams, Ed 77
Williams, Jim 51
Williams-Brice Stadium 171
Williamson, Ivy 231
Williamson, Richard 101
Willingham, Tyrone 181
Willsey, Ray 37
Wilson, Barry 53
Wilson, Kenneth L. 141
Wilson, Shirley "Red" 53
Wilson, Tom 193
Wilson, Wendell 75
Windegger, Frank 195
Winkleman, Ben 169
Winslow, Robert E. 13
Winston-Salem, NC 221
Wisconsin 231
Wise, Harold 147
Witham, Myron 49
Witucki, Bernie 203
Wolf 107, 125, 133
Wolf, Ray "Bear" 59, 130
Wonderling, Tom 229
Wood, William 207
Woodruff, Bob 59, 187
Woods, Sparky 171
Woodson, Warren 13
Woodworth, R.C. 161
Wright, Earl 63
Wyatt, Bowden 17, 187, 233
Wyche, Sam 77
Wyoming 233

Yager Stadium 105
Yard, Rix N. 201
Yeager, Jim 49
Yeoman, Bill 71
Yoshida, Hugh 69
Yost, Fielding 107
Young, Dick 225
Young, James C. 13, 161
Young, Ralph H. 109
Young, Richard 31, 151
Young, Tom 130
Yow, Debbie 99
Ypsilanti, MI 57
Yung, Bill 191
Yurika, Joe 29

Zaunbrecher, Ed 137
Zechman, Fred 129
Zuppke, Bob 75
Zweierlein, Ron 31

www.ingramcontent.com/pod-product-compliance
Ingram Content Group UK Ltd.
Pitfield, Milton Keynes, MK11 3LW, UK
UKHW041937140426
5217IPUK00014B/517